XIXᵗʰ CENTURY
DRAWINGS AND WATERCOLORS

XIXTH CENTURY
DRAWINGS AND WATERCOLORS

BY

JEAN SELZ

CROWN PUBLISHERS INC. · NEW YORK

Translated from the French by
EILEEN B. HENNESSY

LIBRARY OF CONGRESS CATALOG CARD NUMBER 68-9086
PRINTED IN ITALY - © 1968 UFFICIPRESS S.A. LUGANO
ALL RIGHTS IN THE U.S.A. ARE RESERVED BY CROWN PUBLISHERS INC., NEW YORK, N.Y.

FRANCISCO GOYA *Spain* "Es día de su santo" (It's His Name Day)   7
India ink, brush and wash   Cabinet des Dessins, Louvre, Paris

JACQUES LOUIS DAVID *France* Preliminary Sketch for "The Sabine Women" Pencil, pen, and wash Cabinet des Dessins, Louvre, Paris

they conceded to color: its sensuous quality. The supposed opposition between the two modes of expression aroused ideological and scholarly quarrels that date from the seventeenth century. Discussions were held on whether drawing was superior to color, this superiority being that of the intellectual domain over the sensual, as Pierre de Sève attempted to demonstrate during a session of the Académie on March 6, 1677. This was merely an elaboration of the thesis of Charles Le Brun, who had stated that color was "less noble than drawing," since the latter "is purely a creation of the mind." Color was therefore objected to on the grounds of its sensuousness, as if the latter were the characteristic of a lesser art and as if drawing were by definition free from it. Strangely enough, while color was long ago rehabilitated, this opinion of drawing has not yet been completely dispelled. Matisse himself adopted it as his own when he wrote that "Drawing belongs to the domain of the Spirit, color to that of Sensuality."

The potential that drawing possesses to interpret nature by a more or less pronounced linear schematization, in which the heavier (that is, the more purely conventional) the line, the further removed the schematization is from nature, can undoubtedly cause the drawing to seem like an achievement of the mind or, at the very least, as a form of expression that is intermediate between a vision of the mind and an objective observation. But to deny to drawing what is precisely its most remarkable capacity — the ability to reveal by its graphic nature alone that which is in an artist one of the most fertile sources of his creative impulse: his sensuality — would be to disregard the most elementary laws of physical creation.

If there is intellectualization of the form in the mere fact of its reduction to a schematized figure, this intellectualization is not necessarily obtained at the expense of sensibility. The history and even the prehistory of art are not lacking in examples of this coincidence of the synthetical and the palpable; we can observe it in the earliest engravings on bone of the Magdalenian period.

Being the recording instrument of the tangible, and being capable of developing the representation of an idea or an object to the point where it becomes a symbol or sign, drawing can also advance very far in the direction of realistic description. So strong is the power of suggestion of line, however, that we discover the first dawnings of realism in even the most restrained, allusive, and meager sketch. Not many lines are required for the appearance on paper of movement, life, and all those mysterious conjunctures of human nature and the spirit that form what is called character; and the fewer the lines, the stronger our feeling that the artist felt what was unnecessary for our comprehension of his message. These white spaces or *absences* unknown in painting (at least in the painting of an earlier day) are, like the silences in music, the role reserved to us in order that we may penetrate the work offered to our contemplation; the artist has not told or clarified everything, but has left in the construction of the forms a small opening for the entrance of our musings. The images of memory are constructed in this way: they are fragmented, and are always lacking some part that remains invisible in our memory; we could not describe them in their totality, and yet they force themselves upon us with a power of evocation that probably not even the best photographic image would possess. One of the great poetic powers of the drawing is its ability to reveal itself under an aspect that we might consider incomplete but that in truth endows its handwriting with its fundamental intelligence.

STYLE AND TECHNIQUE

Between the rough sketch, whose rapidity excludes the application of any stylistic method, and the carefully executed drawing, in which every line is the product of reflection and which is intended as a complete work in itself, fall the more or less detailed forms of studies that furnish us with information about the working habits of a painter, whether he considers these studies as simple exercises of eye and hand or intends them as the object of his studies toward the preparation of a future painting. The divergence between a project and its realization on canvas is frequent and sometimes considerable, not because of a modification in the composition, but because the spirit and style have changed. This is why a painter's drawings can reveal an aspect of his personality that we do not discover from his paintings. It is interesting to note that while it parallels the history of painting, the history of drawing unfolds on a slightly different esthetic plane, and we shall see that this difference was particularly striking in the nineteenth century. We are led by this difference to recognize the influence that techniques of execution exercise on artists' personalities. All the media regarded as minor in relation to oil painting — ink, watercolor, pastel, and so on — have also had their specialists and their masters, who were not always at ease in other disciplines.

Watercolors and wash drawings frequently occupy in the work of a painter a place intermediate between painting and drawing, and reveal this dual nature when the outlines of the pencil or pen remain visible under the transparent color. The white of the paper sometimes intervenes as a third element with that freedom in which we discover the principle of fragmentation of which we spoke and which, we may note in passing, has been transmitted by the "lesser techniques" to modern painting, which makes great use of nonpainted spaces, that is, of the white space of the canvas.

Most of the older methods continued to be used during the nineteenth century, but the appearance of new materials caused some of them to be relegated to the background. Bister, a combination of gum, glycerine, and the soot of burnt resinous wood, which had been used as a wash for five centuries, was superseded by the discovery, in 1810, of the use of cuttlefish ink (under the name of sepia). At the end of the eighteenth century, new developments in the lead pencil, due to Nicolas Jacques Conté, which were adopted in Austria and Germany by Hardmuth and Faber, made it a tool whose combined precision and softness had been unknown until then. Without the lead pencil, which corresponded so well to his desire for detailed description, Ingres's talent as a prodigious draftsman would probably never have been revealed.

There is nothing to astonish us in the abundance of drawing during the nineteenth century, as revealed by the diversity of its styles even more than by the number of its techniques, if we keep in mind the esthetic evolution of painting from David to Picasso. But such abundance is also due to the fact that this evolution was not reduced, as we might be led to believe by an oversimplified view of the history of art, to a succession of opposing schools beginning with David's neoclassicism. The importance of the role played in painting by the theories of a return to antiquity can be observed only in an essentially French context. What in these theories, for example, had interested Goya? Actually, David was not the only guiding spirit, in his generation, of the future destiny of art. Paralleling "*davidisme*," other currents that had already appeared some thirty years earlier, at the close of the eigh-

JEAN-AUGUSTE-DOMINIQUE INGRES *France* The Montagu Sisters
Pencil Collection Earl of Sandwich Hinchingbrooke, England

teenth century, were developing in Europe. In 1800, David was fifty-two, Goya fifty-four, Füssli fifty-nine. All three belonged to the same generation, and all three represented profoundly different esthetic ideas that are expressed in their drawings with the spontaneity that gives such great value to every form of personal expression.

Goya's joyous or tragic realism (pages 6, 7) and Füssli's romantic dreams (pages 75, 91) had nothing in common with David's love for Greco-Roman antiquity (page 8). It was the latter's good fortune that this fondness corresponded, in advance as it were, with the tastes of the Empire, and more precisely with those of the emperor. He became the painter of the *Sacre* (Coronation) quite naturally, just as he had been the painter of the *Serment des Horaces* (The Oath of the Horatii) before the Revolution; the transition from antiquity to his own age was accomplished with all deference to the traditions of the "noble style."

FROM THE "SABINES" TO THE "CAPRICHOS"

The precision of the pencil or India-ink line in David's drawings reflects his attention to a serious observation of the human body, which, however, would appear in a large composition only in that idealized form that could cause it to look as much like a statue of antiquity as possible. A wash that violently contrasts shadows with the light sometimes gives a theatrical lighting, as in the drawing in the Louvre of *Homère récitant ses vers aux Grecs* (Homer Reciting His Poetry to the Greeks). The painter usually outlined with a wash on the paper his preliminary vision of the large canvases he intended to (but did not always) execute, and thus certain wash drawings furnish us particulars about his abandoned projects. *Le Vieil Horace défendant son fils* (The Elder Horace Defending His Son), for example, is known to us only by a drawing. In addition, it is interesting to see what the ideas that from one drawing to another gradually took shape on paper became on canvas, and how certain movements of figures were clarified and developed to the point where they give the painting its basic rhythm. A phase of one of these movements can be seen in the preliminary sketch for *The Sabines*, drawn by David when he was a political prisoner in a cell of the Luxembourg.

From the window of this prison David painted a *Vue des Jardins du Luxembourg* (View of the Luxembourg Gardens), which is his only known landscape painting; his landscape drawings are almost equally rare. One of these (in the Cabinet des Dessins of the Louvre), a light wash over a pencil sketch touched up with a pen, which represents a Roman scene — *Le Tibre et le Château Saint-Ange* (The Tiber and the Castel Sant'Angelo) — is a rather pretty composition in which, however, we do not feel the love of nature that impregnates the beautiful wash drawings of a Claude Lorrain. David was least of all a landscapist. The precise, vigorous pencil studies by which he "approached," as it were, each figure that was to play a role in his large compositions clearly indicate that he was above all a portraitist. Nevertheless, his painted portraits always had something more conventional about them than did their preliminary sketches. When we look at his quick sketches from life, done in the streets of Paris during the bloody days of the Revolution — those heads impaled on the ends of pikes, or the wretched, tragic silhouette of Marie-

Antoinette seated in the cart carrying her to the scaffold, on which his implacable eye had alighted (as a Deputy to the Convention, David had voted for the death of Louis XVI) — it is impossible to imagine that some twenty years later (in 1814) the same hand would draw the pompous, helmeted nudes of the *Léonidas aux Thermopyles* (Leonidas at Thermopylæ).

Even if the contrast between David and Goya were not so obvious and so clearly demonstrated in their paintings, a comparison of their drawings would suffice to show how far apart they were in both spirit and technique. Both were fond of the beautiful black color of India ink, but whereas David used it with the precision of a stiff pen, Goya brought it to life with the liberty of a supple brush. We encounter this freedom and flexibility, this dexterity of a hand that always hit upon the cruel or satirical line, in hundreds of drawings left by the author of the *Caprichos* (most of which are preserved in the Prado Museum) and which often served him as preliminary drawings for his etchings and lithographs. Very often, however, Goya also drew for the pleasure of drawing, frequently changing his style, utilizing all kinds of washes, and taking an interest in all the activities and classes of humanity.

A painter of pretty women and hags, he was deeply moved by the tragic condition of his country during the invasion by the Napoleonic armies, and his humor became black and savage. The intense realism with which he depicted the horrors of the war found no equivalent in any other European country. At the same period in France — between 1808 and 1815 — the painting of battles was still influenced by the "noble style"; its great lyrical flights told the epics of the conqueror. For Gros (page 18) and Géricault (pages 28, 41) there were no "disasters of war"; there were only heroic deeds. Whether the subject of the painting was *Napoléon sur le champ de bataille d'Eylau* (Napoleon on the Battlefield of Eylau) (Gros) or *Officier de chasseurs à cheval chargeant* (Cavalry Officer Charging) (Géricault), it was completely dominated by the glorification of the hero. The painter attempted, not to look at war, but to transpose it to the level of a new mythology, for the gods of that age wore uniforms. Moreover, for Géricault, the great specialist of horses, every canvas was an opportunity for a splendid equestrian painting.

Later we shall speak about the drawings of these two painters, which reveal an aspect of their personalities not apparent in their paintings. What we wish to stress here is the lucidity of Goya, and the role of witness assigned to the artist by his extraordinary drawings of war. For Goya, drawing could become a protest, a fact that was to impress the mind of more than one artist — and in particular Daumier — during that century. What should be retained, in Goya's work, is not so much the artist's position as a participant in the social struggle, as the action by which art succeeded in achieving a new vision of reality — the preliminary form of a realism that preceded Courbet's *Manifesto* (page 106) by forty years.

MYSTICS AND VISIONARIES

In the middle of the second decade of the century there died in London an elderly artist (he was eighty-four years old in 1825) whose fame in the English capital was sufficient to justify his being buried, despite his Swiss nationality, beside Sir Joshua Reynolds in St. Paul's Cathedral. This artist, who long after his death was still un-

ANTOINE-JEAN GROS (Baron) *France* Equestrian Portrait of Prince Joachim Murat
(Study for " The Battle of Eylau ") Pen drawing École des Beaux-Arts, Paris

ANTOINE-LOUIS BARYE *France* Tiger's Head Charcoal Cabinet des Dessins, Louvre, Paris

known in France, and who had not been well understood in his own country during his lifetime, was Johann Heinrich Füssli. Born in Zurich, in a milieu in which culture went hand in hand with austerity, Füssli, if he had obeyed his father's entreaties, would have entered the ecclesiastical profession. Art exercised a more powerful attraction upon his spirit, however, and although he, like David, at first fell under the spell of Winckelmann's ideas (whose works he translated in London), the idea of "ideal beauty," which he had plenty of leisure to cultivate in the course of his eight-year sojourn in Italy, was to lead him in a completely different direction. He settled down in London in 1781, and began an artistic activity dominated by a partly Elizabethan and partly romantic poetry, in which Shakespeare and Gœthe mingled in strange scenes haunted by the spirit of Michelangelo. He drew on the entire body of fantastic literature for themes for his drawings, unveiling creatures who were only remotely terrestrial: nixies, angels, fairies, phantoms, creatures escaped from *The Song of the Nibelungen*, Dante's *Inferno*, *Paradise Lost*, and Wieland's *Oberon*.

It is easy to understand why William Blake (page 84), who was sixteen years

19

younger than Füssli, was his admirer and friend, and was even influenced by him. The mysticism of the one combined with the symbolism of the other. Both possessed the visionary's conception of art, and the strangeness of their visions, which came closer than any other contemporary form of pictorial expression to a certain type of literary thinking, was a phenomenon which, although isolated, was later to have important repercussions. Today we regard them as precursors, and both were rightly included in the 1965 exhibition of "Several Ancestors of Surrealism" at the Bibliothèque Nationale in Paris. They were in truth among the first explorers of those regions of which Füssli was speaking when he said, "One of the most unexplored regions of Art are dreams."

Blake, who was also an illustrator of Dante, Shakespeare, and Milton, composed series of drawings for Young's *Night Thoughts*, Blair's *The Grave*, and the Bible. His engravings for the *Prophetic Books* were done, he said, by a method revealed to him by his dead brother in the course of an apparition. Such a fact is characteristic of the poet's mind, which was always ready to welcome the intervention of the supernatural. As with Füssli, it was the supernatural, even the demoniac, that attracted him in the stanzas of the *Inferno*. One of his strangest illustrations of Dante is the "Whirlwind of the Lovers," in which male and female bodies are swept up in the gigantic volute of a wave rushing from the shore toward the infinite.

Blake's poetry, moreover, illuminates the demoniac side of the artist. "The star named Blake," André Gide has written, "sparkles in that remote region of the sky in which the star called Lautréamont also shines." Gide praised Blake for having praised Milton: "Blake praised Milton: an authentic poet, he called him, because he was on the side of the devil without realizing it. This is also true of Blake, but he at least realized it. He also knew how to forget the fact: in this lay his strength."

A. G. B. Russell, commenting on the author of the *Marriage of Heaven and Hell*, said that in his drawings he sought a "realism of the imagination." This will also be true, later on and more correctly, of Odilon Redon (pages 108, 109, 110, 111), for Blake's realism never freed itself from a baroque and decorative esthetics that had a distinct tendency to oppose it. While he did not always succeed in playing down the lyrical movements dictated by a similar esthetics, Füssli went much further than Blake in the discovery of these "unexplored regions of art." His strangest and most hallucinated works open new perspectives on certain of the most neglected characteristics of romanticism. The greatest attention has been concentrated on romanticism's most obvious and most theatrical ecstasies; but far more disturbing and mysterious is that which is concealed behind its hidden restlessness.

David, Goya, and Füssli did not all exercise the same influence on the art of their time. We have considered them together here simply because they simultaneously embodied, at the dawn of the nineteenth century, three forms of expression that were sooner or later, whether briefly or with increasing authority, to constitute the most influential movements of artistic creation in the course of the century. While the neoclassicism based on an idealization of nature was to remain without a future, such was not the case for the two other conceptions that opposed the constituents of reality to the resources of the imagination.

These major outlines that dominate the history of painting could serve to establish similar distinctions in the evolution of drawing, but the same names would

EUGÈNE LAMI *France* Four Studies of a Couple Dancing Pencil and wash Cabinet des Dessins, Louvre, Paris

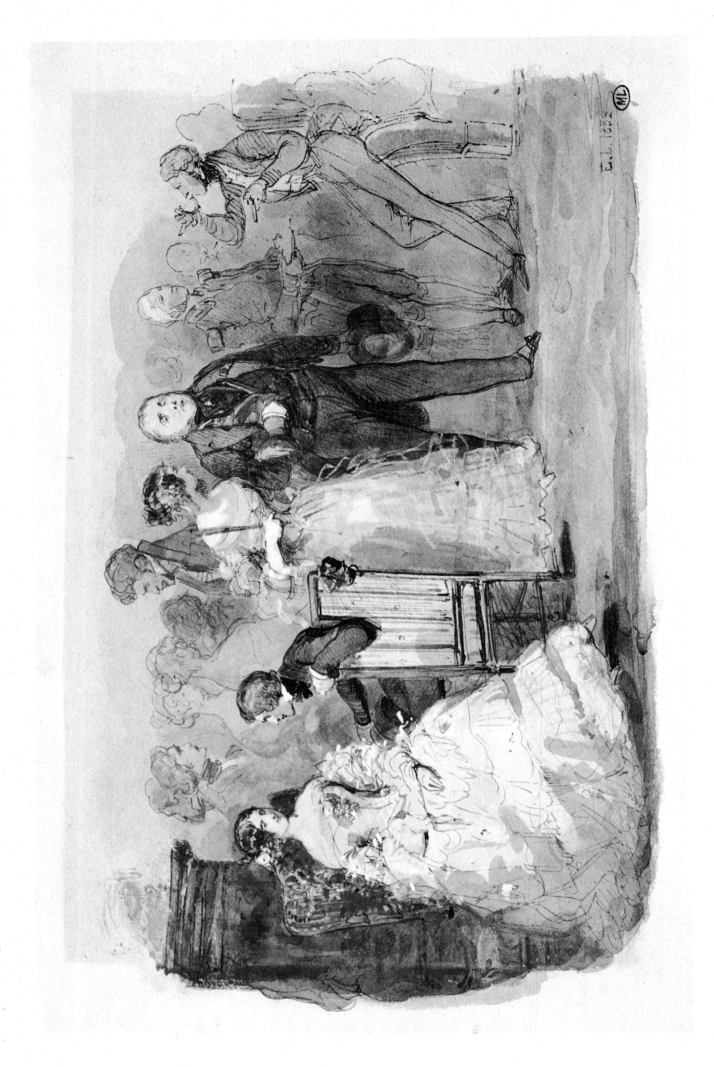

EUGÈNE LAMI *France* A Reception Pen, wash, and watercolor Cabinet des Dessins, Louvre, Paris

GUSTAVE DORÉ. *France* London Fish Seller Watercolor Cabinet des Dessins, Louvre, Paris

not always be found connected with the same tendencies, for a painter who in his canvases remained faithful to classical principles sometimes freed himself from them in his drawings, with a freedom that heralded an approaching change of esthetics. Such was the case with the portraitist Gros. A pupil of David (whose studio was entrusted to his direction in 1816), Gros, having acquired a rigorous academic discipline, became a painter of historic and battle scenes only after personally experiencing the Italian campaign with Bonaparte. This contact with a dramatic reality undoubtedly did not prevent him from trying for somewhat grandiloquent effects in his compositions, but how different is the impression left on us by his drawings. What life and vigor they contain! What daring simplifications in his pen sketches, sometimes tinted with a bister wash, which reveal that he was much more original as a draftsman than as a painter. We could almost see in them the style of Delacroix.

WITH A STROKE OF A PENCIL

In contrast to the foregoing, Ingres (pages 11, 15), another pupil of David, reveals what a close relationship can be established between painting and drawing. The search for a perfect harmony between the two modes of expression seems to have been one of his major preoccupations. The precision of the pencil line and the detailed observation of the smallest detail (a curl of hair, the fold of a ribbon) was equaled by his attention to the coloring of a portrait and the smallest detail of a composition. Looking at one of his canvases, sometimes we even have the impression, when we observe this careful adaptation of painting to drawing, that the painting is only the secondary element, that it is almost superfluous, and presents no technical interest, that it is almost a "coloring process," not an autonomous form of expression. This brings us to the idea that Ingres the painter was inferior to Ingres the draftsman. This combination of precision and delicacy, the delicate modeling of the faces often contrasting with the purely linear drawing of the garments, and the simplicity with which his models posed before him (rather vapidly, as before a photographer), all contributed to the charm of his drawings and helped to endow them with a genuine style — later to be called, and rightly so, *ingresque* — while his canvases, which are dominated by a too obvious desire to charm, seem intended to illustrate, and at the same time to discredit, the idea of classical painting.

The best-known drawings by Ingres are also the most finished ones, those that he executed for his friends or in fulfillment of commissions and that made him famous as a draftsman. Sometimes he grouped an entire family in a single drawing, as in the cases of the Forestier, Stamaty, Guille, and Lucien Bonaparte families (Montauban, Louvre, Bayonne and Fogg Art Museums, respectively). But the studies that served as preliminary sketches for his paintings are less well known; most of them can be seen in the Musée de Montauban, Ingres having left the major portion of his studio to his native city. Its four thousand drawings enable us to follow, section by section, all the slow, careful work done by the artist before painting a canvas: studies of nudes for figures that will later be clothed, a nude model used for preliminary study of poses (a method which he applied even to the portrait of Charles X), studies of garments and details of garments (a shawl, a sleeve, the fold of a tunic), studies of faces, arms, hands, and legs, and sketches of the complete

Bust of Monsieur Guyot   Bust of Monsieur Huguet

JEAN-BAPTISTE ISABEY   *France*   Sepia brush drawing   Kupferstichkabinett, Basel

painting. To prepare a painting like *L'Age d'Or* (The Golden Age), required no fewer than four hundred drawings.

Ingres continued drawing right to the end of his long life. A pencil self-portrait done three years before his death, and preserved in the École des Beaux-Arts in Paris, reveals a certain uneasiness in his gaze — an uneasiness that the artist's eye was nevertheless sufficiently lucid to capture with implacable accuracy. We can also see that the drawing of the garment, with its somewhat wavering lines retouched several times, betrays the advanced age of the artist (he was then eighty-four years old). It is a touching weakness, but one belied by the firmness of this face drawn with a steady hand.

In his pupil Théodore Chassériau (page 38) we discover the same qualities of observation and precision, but the short span of his life — he died at the age of thirty-seven — did not permit him to accomplish so extensive a body of work. He would undoubtedly have become the great portraitist presaged by his beautiful drawings. His pencil portraits, technically very close to those of Ingres, reveal a more obvious sensuality. Despite all that has been written about the author of *Le Bain Turc* (The Turkish Bath), it seems that, in his painting, the eroticism of Ingres was more a stylistic than an emotional matter. Only a great lover like Chassériau could have given his pencil line the kind of caress that envelops his vision of feminine beauty. We know that he was not lacking in women friends — the Countess d'Agoult, Delphine de Girardin, Princess Belgiojoso (of whom he did an admirable portrait in graphite), Princess Marie Cantacuzène, and Alice Ozy, the most beautiful as well as the most diabolical of them all, who gave him much cause for complaint but whom he adored. The *Nymphe endormie* (Sleeping Nymph) (Musée d'Avignon), painted in 1850, in which she is depicted nude, and his pencil portraits of her, help us to understand the fascination that this young woman, whose charms found many admirers (including Victor Hugo), could exercise over the painter.

This special feeling of ardor inspired in Chassériau by feminine beauty — a feeling that was combined with a certain seriousness, and was therefore profoundly different from the *style galant* of the boudoir nudes of the eighteenth century — can also be seen in the best drawings of Prud'hon (pages 5, 13) and Girodet-Trioson (pages 14, 16). The romantic atmosphere exercised its power of idealization without, however, imposing an excessively conventional style of drawing on the forms: the beauty of woman could become poetic without depriving her of her carnal sensibility. It is undoubtedly for this reason that the mythological or literary screen (Psyche or Atala) was still necessary in an art form that was to assign a special place to the feminine body in the history of its pictorial representation, a place intermediate between the neoclassical traditions and the realism of the end of the nineteenth century.

The transition from idealizing romanticism to naturalism thus began to make its presence felt with sufficient persistence to justify our regarding it as a first stage of modern art. Strangely enough, it was just at the time when artists were particularly interested in looking at life in a more objective manner, and were drawing on it for subjects for their works, that art began to become much more subjective; the painter's individuality was revealed and developed in proportion to the immediacy of his confrontation with reality. It is interesting to note that in this spiritual evolution that accompanies the evolution in modes of expression, drawing is very often one step ahead of painting. This seems to be due to the fact that drawing represents a more spontaneous and more immediate technique and that in drawing the artist can assert himself with greater daring and freedom.

STUDIES AND SKETCHES

Thus the distance that separates the draftsman from the painter must be accepted as a major factor in the history of drawing. Histories of art based only on developments in painting (and on these developments as observed in finished works, that is, pictures) fail to take this factor into account, and thus give us a considerably distorted account of the actual evolution of each artist and his deepest (because most impulsive) tendencies, as revealed in his drawings but not always in his paintings. A study of the drawings of the great painters thus obliges us to revise the opinions we may have acquired on the history of art. As an example of this cohabitation of two personalities or, if we prefer, of this dual position that is the ambiguity of a single personality, we shall choose, from the important period in which the principles of a new esthetics were beginning to take form, a famous work by Géricault.

Romanticism undoubtedly posed an obstacle to the birth of naturalism, but already those who were being carried away by its lyrical breath were seeking to adapt it to realistic themes. This was the case with Géricault's *Radeau de la Méduse* (Raft of the Medusa). The subject of this canvas, as is well known, is the tragic event of the shipwreck of a frigate, the *Medusa*, that ran aground in shallow waters on July 2, 1816, while en route to Senegal. A large raft was constructed in an attempt to save the 148 passengers who had not been able to find place in the rowboats. But the rations soon ran short, and the sea became rough. Hunger, exhaustion, madness, and strife transformed the raft into a battlefield of stupid and savage combats. The sailors who died were eaten by the survivors. This nightmare continued for ten days. When a brig arrived to pick up the shipwrecked victims, only fourteen were still alive. The pathetic character of such a horrifying situation inspired Géricault with a composition that is not lacking in grandeur. But if we compare the finished canvas, which was exhibited at the Salon of 1819, with the preliminary drawings, we cannot fail to be struck by the contrasts between the carefully composed painting and its preparatory studies, which reveal a search for truth rather than a search for style.

These studies include a series of more or less carefully developed drawings for each group and for each figure, and a large, partially painted, fairly complete sketch in which, however, most of the figures (more numerous than in the final composition) remained in the state of drawings. Moreover, in his desire to approach his subject with a genuinely realistic vision, the painter went to the Hôpital Beaujon to draw corpses, as he was later to go to the Salpêtrière to do studies of the insane. Several of these studies can be seen at the Musée Bonnat in Bayonne, which houses 119 of Géricault's drawings.

The sketch, which may be considered a first version of the *Radeau*, undoubtedly appears less harmonious in construction than the canvas, for the latter is composed with a calculated precision, and we may say that its rhythm and geometry achieve a kind of perfection. It differs in many ways from the arrangement of the sketch: the movement of the sea is more surging, there is an emphasis in size and importance on the triangle formed by the human pyramid of the victims; the gesture of the two men moving their arms, to whose hands a rag is tied as a signal, is more effective, and so on. But all this adds nothing to the poignant truth of the drama. On the contrary, a tendency to force the tone slightly, to make it more lyrical by an obvious search for eloquent gestures and dramatic poses, gives the painting a somewhat theatrical appearance that weakens its anguished quality. The real dramatic power of the *Radeau* and the most original work done by Géricault are found in the drawings and sketches. The realistic draftsman had let himself be carried away by the romantic painter.

His drawings, several landscape studies, and projects for paintings that he was never to execute permit us to suppose that Géricault would have evolved in a direction that is not foreshadowed in his painting. But destiny did not give him time to continue his work: like Chassériau, he died prematurely in 1824, at the age of thirty-three, as the result of a fall from a horse. (Decamps [page 45] died in similar fashion: he was thrown by his mount against a tree.) This fatal passion for horses also provided Géricault with a major portion of his work, for his knowledge of the horse was not simply that of a rider. He undoubtedly acquired his fondness for drawing horses from Carle Vernet, with whom he worked in his youth. His studies of skeletons and anatomical models even resulted in a famous sculpture, the *Anatomie du cheval*. We know from his numerous drawings that he was interested in all kinds of horses — thoroughbreds, racehorses, draft animals, the latter sometimes harnessed to carts or artillery caissons — which reappear in his lithographs and canvases. Beautiful wash drawings and watercolors on these themes are preserved in the Musée Bonnat, the Chicago Art Institute, and the Wadsworth Atheneum in Hartford, Connecticut; the latter houses the *Chariot de charbon* (The Coal Wagon), one of the subjects drawn by Géricault during his stay in England, which was to appear in one of the lithographs of his *Suite anglaise*, published in 1821.

While the horse made its first appearance in battle scenes (in which it was to play an important role in the works of Delacroix), it was in a more peaceful but equally persistent form that it came to occupy first place in nineteenth-century drawing, where it appeared along with jockeys, riders, and horsewomen in the works of Alfred de Dreux and Constantin Guys (pages 42, 43, 44), and became, together with dancers, the favorite theme of Degas.

THÉODORE GÉRICAULT *France* Study of Horses
Pen drawing Detroit Institute of Art

GRANDVILLE (Jean Gérard) *France* Birdmen
Graphite   Collection R. R., Paris

GENESIS OF A PAINTING

It is in the works of Delacroix (pages 32, 33, 34, 35) that we find the most highly developed and most powerful form of this realism sublimed by romanticism, the first revelations of which we saw in the works of Géricault. Most of the numerous drawings we have from Delacroix's hand are studies for his large compositions, but this is not to say that he despised ink or watercolor paintings as "minor techniques." Several figures of women (like the pretty sepia drawing of *Marie Kalergis au piano*) and landscapes for example, (the watercolors of the *Falaises d'Étretat* — The Cliffs of Étretat) are small, complete works in themselves. But the preoccupation — we might say the obsession — aroused in him by the execution of the large canvases that he sent to the Salon, or the major decorative works commissioned from him, was translated by unremitting toil, that is, in numerous pencil, pen, wash, watercolor, and sometimes pastel studies. These furnish us with valuable information about the manner in which the first idea for a painting came into his mind, and how the figures that were to appear in it, singly and in groups, gradually took definite shape.

The process of this slow development can be followed in an interesting fashion in the *Massacres de Scio* (The Massacres of Chios), painted in 1824, the drawings for which are so many elements that permit us to analyze this canvas and to admire the mastery with which Delacroix, at the age of twenty-six, could develop a work to its most perfect and most tragic form.

29

FRANÇOIS-MARIUS GRANET *France* The Cloister of Santa Maria del Popolo
Sepia wash Besançon Museum, Besançon

ACHILLE DEVÉRIA *France* Portrait of a Woman
Graphite Ecole des Beaux-Arts, Paris

EUGÈNE DELACROIX *France* The Daughter of Abraham-ben-Chimol and Her Servant
Charcoal Collection Walter Cummings Baker, New York

EUGÈNE DELACROIX *France* Study of a Jewess
Watercolor Fabre Museum, Montpellier

Eugène Delacroix *France* Study for "The Massacre of Scio"
Watercolor Cabinet des Dessins, Louvre, Paris

34

The painter, who was particularly sensitive to everything concerning the world of the East, had been profoundly moved by the conflict that since 1820 had been pitting the Greeks and the Turks against each other. The desire to express in a work of art the feelings aroused in him by this struggle for Greek independence had not been satisfied by his two watercolors on this theme. The shocking tragedy of Chios, in August, 1822, where almost twenty thousand inhabitants of this island were massacred by the Turks, and the women were carried off into slavery, haunted him until he made it the subject of a painting.

Through his *Journal* we are able to follow the manner in which this work, to which he was to devote seven months of preliminary studies, was executed. Several of these studies are preserved in the Cabinet des Dessins of the Louvre. There is first a pen sketch, in which a tangle of bodies and indistinct silhouettes of horses, hardly discernible, emerge from a confused, almost abstract mass. From this schematic initial drawing we can already understand what movement Delacroix was trying to give his composition: an arrangement of figures of women and warriors supported, as it were, on the flank of a charger. In other drawings the poses of the principal figures are roughed out in pencil sketches: the old woman seated on the ground, whom we see in the foreground of the canvas; the woman leaning on the shoulder of a dying man; and the beautiful captive tied to a horse. The painter had decided on the latter's position (posed for by a model and close friend of Delacroix named Émilie Robert) before determining the arrangement of the groupings in the composition. In the watercolor that served him as a preliminary version (and which was later modified considerably), she looks much as we have already seen her in the sketches, and as she will appear in the final version: her arms raised, her face concealed, and her magnificent naked body forming a striking contrast to the rather morbid character of the scene, in which the wounded and the dying are mingled. Thus Delacroix had planned this contrast right from the initial conception of the *Massacres de Scio*, and it was to form the most gripping portion of the painting.

Thus an examination of studies sheds light on an artist's creative process. Through them we learn of his intentions, his hesitations, and the fundamental ideas in which lies the key to his work. In the case of Delacroix they also enable us to compare the work of the painter with that of the novelist, who gathers his material by taking notes on real life with which he will flesh out the fiction of his books. Many are the sketches brought back by the painter from his travels in Morocco, Algeria, and Spain, which he was to utilize in his large compositions. We shall see these Arabs and Jewesses, and these odalisques drawn in a harem that he had obtained permission to visit, reappear in more than one canvas (for example, in the *Noce Juive* — The Jewish Wedding — and the two versions of the *Femmes d'Alger* — Women of Algeria), just as we shall discover in his landscapes the tigers and lions he went to draw in front of their cages in the Jardin des Plantes. There he sometimes found himself in the company of Barye (page. 19), whose watercolor studies of wild animals have become as famous as his sculptures. Watercolor, admirably utilized by Delacroix for his quick sketches, also served him for very detailed studies. To the Count de Mornay, whom he accompanied on his mission to the Sultan Abd-er RahmanII, he made a gift of eighteen watercolors done during this trip to Morocco in 1832; they are now dispersed in various collections.

THÉODORE CHASSÉRIAU *France* Moorish Woman
Pencil   Cabinet des Dessins, Louvre, Paris

HENRI REGNAULT *France* Anatomical Study
Charcoal Besançon Museum, Besançon

WATERCOLORS AND LANDSCAPES

French taste for the watercolor has always been sporadic in its manifestations. In the eighteenth century, the passing interest taken in it by Boucher, Fragonard, and such engravers as the brothers Saint-Aubin or Moreau the elder, was far surpassed by enthusiasm for the pastel. Treated in a quasi-pictorial fashion, it seemed the most appropriate technique for the portrait. The sanguine drawing, valued for its soft appearance, was also in great favor, as was the combination of the carbon pencil, chalk, and sanguine on buff or blue-tinted paper. At the turn of the eighteenth century few artists in France utilized the watercolor for anything more than color notes on sketches for paintings or for illustrations in the field of natural history. Here the watercolor found its master in the person of Pierre-Joseph Redouté (1759-1840) (page 56), whose name is today inseparable from the hundreds of roses he drew for the purpose of recording the botanical characteristics of each species. His pictures of flowers and fruit are remarkable not only for the exacting observation that guided their execution but also for the delicacy and grace of their technique.

Another famous watercolor artist was Jean-Baptiste Isabey (1767-1855) (page 25), a miniaturist and the official portraitist of the Empire. His personality is of secondary interest, however, when compared with that of a less renowned artist who may nevertheless be regarded as the best watercolorist of his time: François-Marius Granet (1775-1849) (pages 30, 104). A pupil of David, but more strongly influenced by Rembrandt, Granet became known particularly for his views of monuments and his monastic scenes. The best examples of his work are found in his small landscapes with their highly individualistic coloring, in which his great sensitivity is expressed with rare austerity of means, Many of his works are housed in the museum that bears his name in his native city of Aix-en-Provence.

Only with the stir created by the English school, however, did the watercolor find enthusiastic practitioners in France. The situation in England was different, and for quite some time — in fact, since the middle of the eighteenth century — landscapists there had been specializing in the watercolor. The first artist to utilize it systematically was Paul Sandby (1725-1809), who was also responsible for the introduction of the aquatint into England. Some thirty of his watercolors and gouaches can be seen in the Victoria and Albert Museum in London. The romantic landscape, apparently born in Italy and Switzerland, first appeared in England in the watercolors of John Robert Cozens (1752-1797), who had traveled in both countries in the company of William Beckford, a strange individual and the author of *Vathek*. The melancholy lakes, cypress trees, and steep, rocky sites, done in blue-gray monochrome, were to play a major role in the school of watercolorists founded by Dr. Thomas Monro — the Monro School — in which the works of Cozens were given to the pupils to be copied, and which was attended by Thomas Girtin, John Sell Cotman, John Varley, Peter de Wint, and William Turner, all well-known landscapists in England. Later on, we shall speak about Turner, whose personality was to dominate this entire group.

The history of the English landscape is thus linked with the history of the watercolor, which also has its "genre painters," like Thomas Rowlandson (page 71), who belongs to a tradition of humor and social satire, between Hogarth and Gillray, and who enjoyed great popularity thanks to his caricatures. But the strongest proof

THÉODORE GÉRICAULT *France* View of Montmartre   Pen, sepia and watercolor   Collection Claude Aubry, Paris

42

CONSTANTIN GUYS *France* Riders in the Bois
Watercolor Cabinet des Dessins, Louvre, Paris

CONSTANTIN GUYS *France* Woman with Basket
Watercolor Musée du Petit Palais, Paris

43

CONSTANTIN GUYS *France* Reception at Court
Watercolor Cabinet des Dessins, Louvre, Paris

44

ALEXANDRE-GABRIEL
DECAMPS
France
Woman Walking,
Basket and Jug
Charcoal
with touches
of white gouache
Besançon Museum
Besançon

45

STANISLAS LÉPINE
France
Woman's Head
Charcoal
Cabinet des Dessins
Louvre, Paris

46

ADOLPHE
MONTICELLI
France
Valet with
a Greyhound
Graphite
Kupferstichkabinett
Basel

47

JEAN-FRANÇOIS MILLET *France* Seated Peasant Woman Holding a Sheaf
Charcoal Besançon Museum, Besançon

48

of the importance acquired by the English watercolorists very early in the nineteenth century is the founding, in 1804, of their society, The Society of Painters in Water-Colours (later better known under the title of the Old Water-Colour Society). The artists who founded this association thus proclaimed their desire for independence by remaining aloof from the Royal Academy, where, dissatisfied with their role as poor relations, they thenceforth refrained from exhibiting.

Two of the most interesting artists of this generation were Peter de Wint (1784-1849) and David Cox (1783-1859), the latter a pupil of John Varley, who can be considered a precursor, less inspired than Turner, of impressionism. It was John Constable, however, who exercised the strongest influence on French painting. This may seem surprising to us, for we cannot easily transport ourselves in thought to the position of the men of 150 years ago in order to look at painting. To us, Constable's work seems to be completely lacking in what constitutes the strength of an engaging personality; to our eyes, it contains only a peaceful confrontation of the painter with nature, the honest testimony of the love of a man, without esthetic anguish, for the beautiful trees and meadows of his native land. This is exactly what was missing, however, in the idealist-theoreticians of the beautiful: they had succeeded in creating an artificial world, and no longer knew how to look at nature simply, to look at it for itself, and not for the setting it might furnish for a historical or mythological scene.

JEAN-FRANÇOIS MILLET   *France*   Study for " The Gleaners "
Graphite   Louvre, Paris

This is why the discovery of the English landscape at the Salon of 1824, at which Constable exhibited, was such a revelation for the Parisian painters. Among those most profoundly and durably impressed was Eugène Delacroix.

A PRECURSOR OF ABSTRACTION

For us, however, in the context of our twentieth-century vision, not Constable (page 70) but Turner (pages 64, 81, 82) is the greatest English landscapist of this period. Born in 1775 — one year earlier than Constable — Turner at the age of fifteen exhibited his first watercolors at the Royal Academy, of which he became a member at the age of twenty-seven. We possess some beautiful youthful drawings from his hand, in particular those which he brought back in large numbers (some five hundred) from his first trip to France and Switzerland in 1802. Without the knowledge of his later works, however, we should never have known him as such an outstanding colorist and extraordinary watercolor painter, for it was in his later years that his most original personality was revealed. Italy, where he stayed for the first time in 1819, was probably at the origin of the experiments that were later (beginning around 1830) to lead him to the dissolving concept of color that ultimately caused the explosion, so to speak, of the entire structure of a landscape into light. Some of his biographers, feeling that Turner went too far in sacrificing form to color, have reproached him for this development. But it is precisely on this account that he achieved his most original work, and attained to that poetic power that John Ruskin recognized in him. It also made him much more than a precursor of impressionism, for he went further than any of the impressionist painters in the perception of objects subjected to the action of light. It could truthfully be said of him that he was a precursor of abstraction.

It is in Turner's watercolors that we find the most spontaneous evidence of his evolution. Those done at Lake Lucerne (1830) and Venice (around 1839), and the watercolor of *The Burning of the Houses of Parliament in 1834* (the former are in the British Museum, which also houses his first drawing done at the age of twelve; the latter is in the National Gallery) are among the most remarkable works known in this technique, in which he was unequaled.

While he never attained to equal stature, and although he was particularly noted as a portraitist, the Hungarian painter Miklós Barabás (1810-1898) (page 83), whose works bear the stamp of the Biedermeier style, displayed in some of his youthful landscapes a concept of the watercolor that allies him to a certain extent with Turner. His works reveal a similar delicacy in the tonal relationships, and a similar refinement of colored forms.

After Turner's death (which occurred on December 19, 1851), in addition to three hundred oil paintings, nineteen thousand watercolors, drawings, and pages of sketches were found in his studio. Despite its importance, however, the influence of Turner's work did not immediately cross the Channel. It was preceded by the work of Richard Parkes Bonington (page 62), who was better known in France. (It is true that he had come with his family to live in that country at an early age). His brief association with the studio of Gros was less profitable to him than his valuable friendship with Delacroix. It was by his watercolors that Bonington first became

THÉODORE ROUSSEAU *France* Landscape
Pen drawing, India ink Collection F., Paris

known, and helped to encourage a reawakening of interest in a technique that
had been somewhat neglected in France. He utilized the technique to its best
advantage, exercising great subtlety in the play of transparencies, and his spontaneity
of execution often led him to paint directly with the brush, without preliminary
drawing. The landscapes he brought back from his sojourns in Verona, Venice,
and Normandy, or in his own country, convinced more than one artist that the
watercolor was not a negligible form of expression. This influence of the young
English painter is all the more remarkable because his body of work is a small one:
he died in London in 1828, still in his twenties.

Despite his professed admiration for Bonington, Corot (pages 52, 53) never
became interested in watercolor painting. This is not true of the landscape artists
who formed, around the person of Théodore Rousseau (pages 51, 54), the Barbizon
School. From the hand of Rousseau himself we have interesting watercolor drawings
(preserved in the Louvre and the Musée Fabre in Montpellier). They are the work
of a sensitive observer of nature, and represent a step forward in the progressive
abandonment by painters of the "studio landscape." Daubigny (page 55), too, was

JEAN-BAPTISTE CAMILLE COROT *France* Little Girl with a Beret
Graphite Musée des Beaux-Arts, Lille

THÉODORE ROUSSEAU *France* The King's Highway
Charcoal and watercolor Cabinet des Dessins, Louvre, Paris

CHARLES DAUBIGNY *France* Landscape ▷
Graphite Cabinet des Dessins, Louvre, Paris

54

VENTE
COROT

JEAN-BAPTISTE CAMILLE COROT *France* Woman at the Bedside of a Child
Charcoal and stump Cabinet des Dessins, Louvre, Paris

VICTOR HUGO *France* Romantic Landscape with Castle and Arched Bridge
Pen drawing, India ink   Kupferstichkabinett, Basel

an outdoor landscapist, and his favorite riverbanks and ponds would later reappear, in a different form, in the works of the impressionists. He had set up a studio on his boat, the *Botin*, on which he traveled up and down the Seine. He made use of the many pen drawings depicting scenes of river life, and quick sketches from life which he accumulated during his travels, in the engraving of a series of etchings which he published in a collection entitled *Voyage en bateau*.

In the same period (around 1860), Henri Harpignies was still painting, finding in watercolor and wash techniques a form of expression that revealed a particularly interesting aspect of his personality (page 92, 127). What was still conventional and somewhat cold in his painting appeared in these works to be swept away in a greater liberty of vision and treatment. In his landscapes, with their simplified masses, mysterious nature led the eye to an absorbing contemplation.

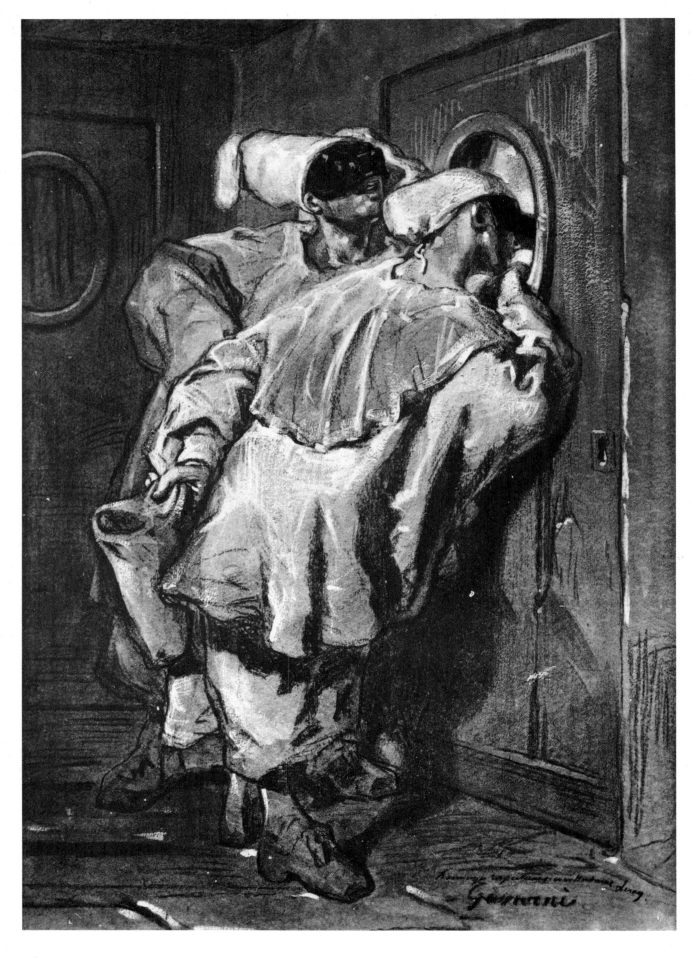

60   Gavarni (Guillaume-Sulpice Chevalier) *France* Two Clowns
Cabinet des Dessins, Louvre, Paris

GAVARNI (Guillaume-Sulpice Chevalier) *France* Portrait of Madame d'Abrantès
Graphite and watercolor Cabinet des Dessins, Louvre, Paris

RICHARD PARKES BONINGTON *England* View of the English Coast
Watercolor Former Collection Majowsky, Museum of Fine Arts, Budapest

James Abbot McNeill Whistler *United States* Stormy Sunset
Pastel with touches of gouache Fogg Art Museum, Cambridge, Massachusetts

JOSEPH MALLORD WILLIAM TURNER *England* Sunset on the Grand Canal of Venice Watercolor British Museum, London

DUTCH CANALS AND THE BEACHES OF NORMANDY

The two artists who made the greatest contributions, after the English, to the entrance of the watercolor into the history of painting in the nineteenth century were Johan Barthold Jongkind (pag. 112) and Eugène Boudin (page 126). The former came to Paris from Holland in 1846, at the age of twenty-seven, and worked for a short time with Isabey. But the coolness of such a master was hardly suited to Jongkind, who was attracted by landscape, of which he had a very vivid conception. The nervous style of his drawings and the animated strokes of his watercolors (a reflection of his unstable nature) epitomize a style to which he remained faithful throughout his life. He painted particularly in France, and made several sojourns in Switzerland, Belgium, and Holland. He never made any major trips, but was continually on the move from Amsterdam to Marseille, from Brest to Grenoble. It has been found that the cities in which he worked, and from which he brought back collections of small landscapes, total fifty-eight.

He attained fame particularly through his seascapes, although all kinds of scenery can be found in his work: the canals and windmills of his native land, frozen ponds over which skaters are gliding, roads on the outskirts of villages, rivers at sunset, and so on. His streets of Paris under snow, and his scenes of small provincial cities or suburbs, are stamped with a sensitivity that points to Utrillo. Unfortunately, this was not Jongkind's only affinity with the painter of Montmartre: he also shared the latter's alcoholism. A sick man, and a prey to mental troubles, worry, and hallucinations, he came to a pitiful end.

Eugène Boudin was an admirer of Jongkind, and immediately fell under his influence, often painting in the same places — at Honfleur and on the beaches of Normandy. For a time the anecdotal side of his painting detracted attention from the interest of his technique, and because of his *Plages de Trouville*, in which women in crinoline strolled under their parasols in attractive groupings on the sand, he was regarded as the painter of the elegant middle class of the Second Empire, and specifically of the middle class on vacation. When justice was done to the value of his individuality, his quality as a colorist, and the freshness of his impressions, he was recognized as one of the first impressionists, and in exhibiting at their first Salon in 1874 he found his rightful place.

While Boudin often painted on the Normandy coast, of which he was particularly fond (he was born in Honfleur, and died at Deauville), he also worked in Brittany, the south of France, Belgium, and Holland. He was almost seventy when he discovered Venice. His work as a watercolor painter has placed him among the great painters in this technique. His pastels, though numerous, are less well known, but demonstrate that in this field also he had acquired a freedom and strength of expression that made him much more than a minor talent.

We shall later see how the watercolor, involved in the new movements in painting, took on new forms at the end of the century. Let us first go back and examine, within the context of the landscapists, what the simple pencil was to one of the greatest among them.

AN INGRES OF THE LANDSCAPE

Corot kept most of his drawings (which were numerous) in his studio until the day he died. They were then dispersed on the auction block at a posthumous sale, at the Hôtel Drouot, in May of 1875. The incomplete *catalogue raisonné* of his work, drawn up by Alfred Robaut in 1905, inventories 577 of them, exclusive of his 85 sketchbooks. Approximately half of these drawings are today in the Louvre; some very beautiful ones can also be found in the Musée Wicar in Lille (including the famous *Petite fille au béret*, which bears such a striking resemblance to a drawing by Holbein) and in American museums (including the Chicago Art Institute and the Fogg Art Museum at Harvard).

In contrast to what we have observed in the works of Gros, and sometimes of Géricault, in Corot's evolution his purely graphic esthetics closely followed the development of his pictorial esthetics. (We shall later see that this was also true of Van Gogh.) In this case, painter and draftsman were one and the same artist. In painting, Corot's work can be divided into two major periods that constitute two manners or two styles. The first took form during his first stay in Italy, from 1825

JAMES WARD *England* Injured Tiger
Pencil and watercolor British Museum, London

GASPAR DAVID FRIEDRICH *Germany*
Young Man Sitting by a Roadmark in the Form of a Gravestone   77
Pen drawing in India ink, wash   Staatliche Graphische Sammlung, Munich

JOHN SINGLETON COPLEY   *United States*   Woman and Child in Flight
Graphite and white chalk   Museum of Fine Arts, Boston, Massachusetts

WINSLOW HOMER *United States* Fishing for Herring Black and white chalks Cooper Union Museum, New York

in Gavarni's handwriting, in one corner of the sketch, betrays a strange anguish that is at variance with the reputation for optimism ascribed to him by his commentators: "One should love nothing and become attached to nothing, for sooner or later we must leave everything behind."

Beginning in 1830, Gavarni collaborated on *La Mode*, a paper published by Émile de Girardin, and then on *Le Diable à Paris*, published by Pierre Hetzel in 1845. His *Œuvres choisies*, "studies of contemporary morals," was published by Hetzel between 1846 and 1848, in 80 instalments that cost 50 centimes each; Théophile Gautier wrote the introduction to the series. Hetzel, the publisher of Balzac, George Sand, Stendhal, Victor Hugo, and later Jules Verne, was the great disseminator of the illustrated book, and it was principally for him and for his edition of *La Comédie Humaine* that such artists as Gavarni, Henry Monnier, Tony Johannot, Meissonier, Bertall, and others, worked.

But the man who by his spirit and imagination stands out from this group of artists, and who has a place among the precursors of an imagery of the subconscious, was Grandville (1803-1847), whose real name was Jean Gérard. For him, drawing was a genuine tool for the exploration of a beyond-the-real that, as has often been stressed, foreshadowed the visions of surrealism. A light irony guided his pencil through a universe of metamorphoses in which the absurd and the supernatural united in oneiric apparitions. His graphic divagations on *Les Cannes* (The Canes), *Les Parapluies* (The Umbrellas), *Les Pipes* (The Pipes), *Les Chapeaux* (The Hats), *Les Etoiles* (The Stars), and his *Scènes de la vie privée et publique des animaux* (Scenes of the Public and Private Life of Animals) (the texts for which were written in 1842 by Balzac, Charles Nodier, George Sand, and Alfred de Musset, among others), the illustrations for his *Fleurs animées* (Animated Flowers), and especially those for *Un autre monde* (Another World), open our eyes to the correspondence that can exist between artistic expression and the mechanisms of thought. By associations of forms analogous to associations of ideas, he transposed the suggestions of poetic language into the visual domain. Very few people then were able to perceive Grandville's originality of spirit or recognize the value of his esthetic suggestions. His wife herself attached so little importance to his drawings that she used them for curl-papers. Grandville died in an insane asylum at the age of forty-four.

In the following generation, that of the 1830's, Gustave Doré (pages 23, 87) also utilized his great talent as a draftsman in the service of the illustrated book. Among his publishers we again encounter the name of Hetzel; it was he who in 1861 published Perrault's fairy tales with forty drawings by Doré. It was exceptional, however, for Doré to agree to work on a children's book, for his enthusiasm and dramatic imagination were better expressed in the illustration of such works as *Don Quixote*, Dante's *Inferno*, or the *Mythologie du Rhin*. He also collaborated on editions of the works of Rabelais and Ariosto, and the Bible. Doré had a great capacity for work, and was never lacking in invention. His drawings are counted in the thousands, but his watercolors are less well known. They are curious in that they reveal a direct observation of nature, whether in scenes of daily life sketched in London or other cities in which Gustave Doré lived, or in landscapes in which the artist seems to have suddenly forgotten the drawing of the objects to retain only their color, spread out in large, simplified masses that are in contrast to his customary work.

REAL LIFE IN PICTURES

If we have not included Daumier (pages 123, 125) in this constellation of artists whose contribution to nineteenth-century book illustration has just been briefly outlined, it is because his work far surpasses that of an illustrator. There is no doubt that his fame during his lifetime was due to his collaboration on newspapers, and it was in *La Silhouette*, the first illustrated satirical weekly published in France, that he made his debut. Thus it is fitting that his name is as closely connected with the history of drawing as with that of journalism. But Daumier was also a great painter and an inspired sculptor, and if he had been satisfied merely to paint and sculpt, undoubtedly he would not have wanted for glory; it would merely have come to him a little later, and have been less popular. In any case, here we are speaking only of his drawings.

JOSEPH MALLORD WILLIAM TURNER *England* South Side of the Piazza San Marco
Watercolor British Museum, London

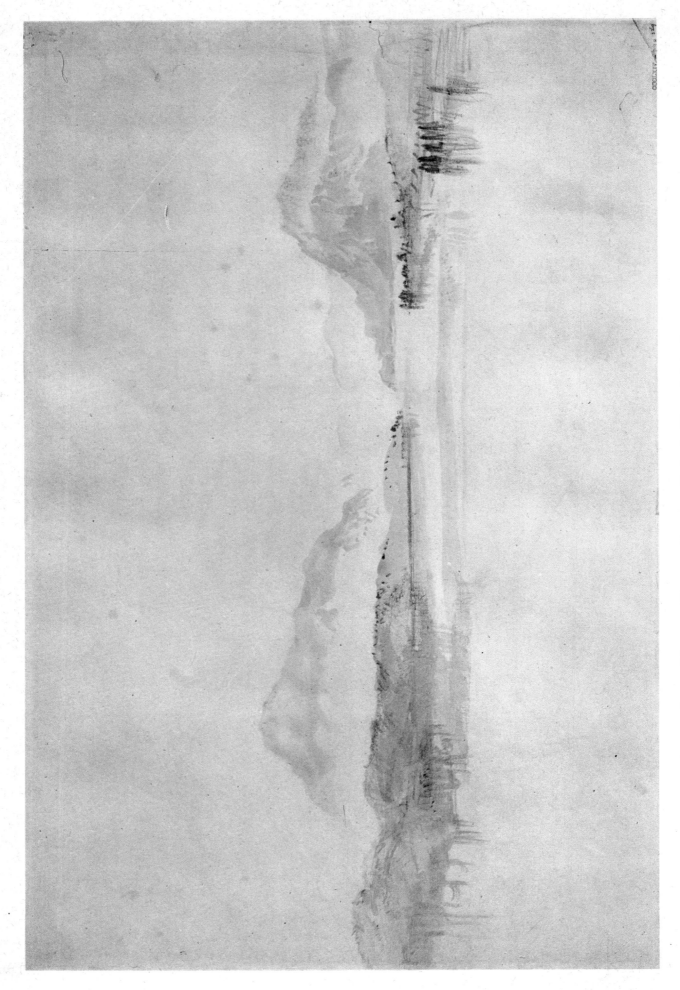

Joseph Mallord William Turner *England* View of Lake Lucerne
Watercolor British Museum, London

MIKLÓS BARABÁS *Hungary* Lake Maggiore Watercolor Museum of Fine Arts, Budapest

HELL
Canto 19

WILLIAM BLAKE *England* The Simoniac Pope Illustration for Dante's *Divine Comedy*
Watercolor Tate Gallery, London

RODOLPHE BRESDIN *France* Clump of Trees
Pen, India ink Collection Galerie Le Bateau-Lavoir, Paris

ECCE

VICTOR HUGO *France*
Ecce Wash, India ink Former Collection of Franz Liszt Museum of Fine Arts, Budapest

GUSTAVE DORÉ *France* Nocturnal Brawl Outside a Pub
Brush, Indian ink and gouache Kupferstichkabinett, Basel

He began his long artistic career as a caricaturist. Being contemptuous of social institutions, and not hesitant to exercise his biting wit to the detriment of the monarchy, he was the perfect choice for *La Caricature*, the subversive newspaper founded by Charles Philipon, on which Balzac collaborated, and which published 251 numbers between 1830 and 1835. Here Daumier found himself in the company of Devéria, Henry Monnier, Grandville, Raffet, Paul Huet, and others. The series of his thirty-eight drawings on *Les Gens de Justice* (Men of Law) appeared in *Le Charivari* between 1845 and 1848.

Daumier, ironically contemptuous of the middle class, attacked the entire social structure that was its mainstay and its pride. Magistrates, doctors, politicians, professors, and landlords were the victims of his savage pen and the burlesque heros of his famous series of lithographs that, under various titles (*Les Cent Robert Macaire* (The Hundred Robert Macaires), *Les Types parisiens* (Parisian Types). *Les Mœurs conjugales* (Conjugal Morals), *Les Bas-bleus* (The Bluestockings), and so on, portrayed a veritable *Comédie Humaine*.

Daumier executed no fewer than 4,000 lithographs; in relation to the number of other works he left, they represent his most important accomplishment. It is, however, his pen and wash (and occasionally carbon pencil) drawings that reveal the greatest originality and in which he expressed himself with that freedom and power that before his time could be found only in a Rembrandt or a Goya. In addition, he had a very personal manner of using watercolor, and of combining with the colors an India-ink wash, thus obtaining a dark coloring supported by the black lines of his drawing.

Being endowed with a rare visual memory, Daumier could draw the most exact portrait likeness without the aid of even the smallest sketch. In this way he executed the small clay busts of politicians that later served him as models for his lithographs and that, by the daring energy of their modeling, are a milestone in the history of modern sculpture.

Constantin Guys possessed a similar type of memory, and he too was for a part of his life associated with journalism; he was for a long time a correspondent for the *Illustrated London News*, and even a war correspondant, since it was through his reports and drawings that this magazine followed the Crimean campaign. His impressions of the battle of Balaklava and his views of military encampments in Turkey are in strange contrast to his often frivolous scenes of Parisian life that won for him his most durable fame. We find in both types, however, the same lively observation; and his technical skill is in perfect harmony with that eagerness of gaze that caused Baudelaire, his friend and biographer, to say that "curiosity can be considered the foundation of his genius."

Guys was never a painter in the generally accepted sense of the term, that is, implying the practice of oil painting. But while he always preferred to express himself through the media of the wash drawing and the watercolor, the originality of his work and his eyewitness reports on the pomps and pleasures of the Second Empire completely justify the title of Baudelaire's series of articles on him in *Le Figaro* of November and December, 1863 — "The Painter of Modern Life."

"Often bizarre, violent, and outrageous, but always poetic, he was able to concentrate in his drawings the bitter or heady flavor of the wine of Life" — so

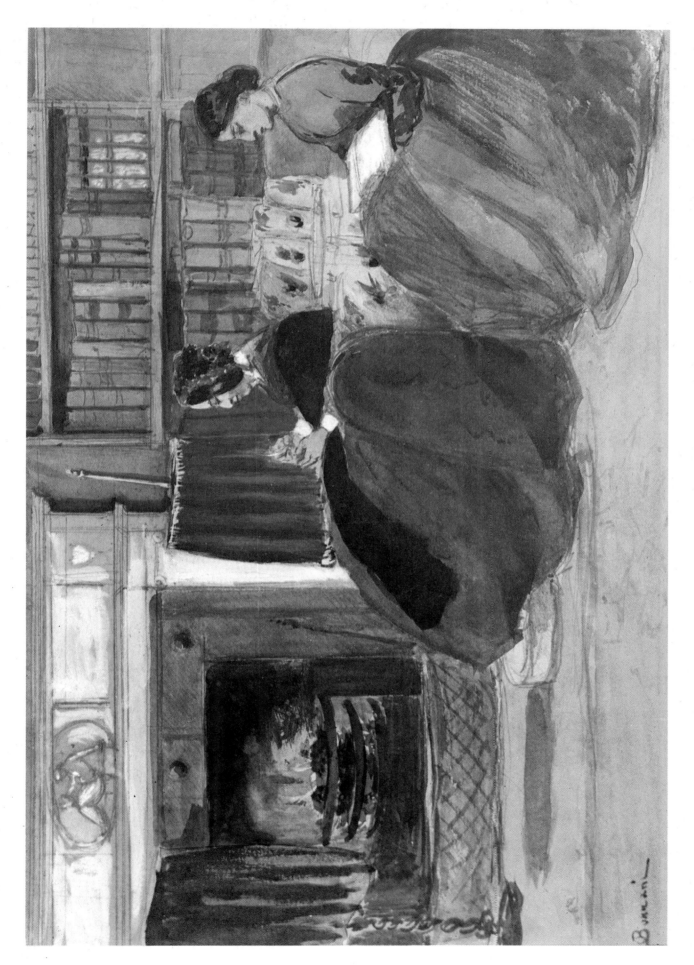

ODOARDO BORRANI *Italy* The Reading Period Watercolor on cardboard Collection Carlo Grassi, Galleria d'Arte Moderna, Milan

GIOVANNI BOLDINI *Italy* Woman with a Muff
Watercolor Private collection, Geneva

JOHANN HEINRICH FÜSSLI *Switzerland* Nude
Watercolor British Museum, London

91

HENRI HARPIGNIES *France* Landscape with Mediterranean Sea in Background
Watercolor Musée du Petit Palais, Paris

HENRY MONNIER *France* A Young Woman ▷
Watercolor Collection Gosselin, Paris

GUSTAVE MOREAU
France
Study for Salomé
Pen, India ink
Musée Gustave Moreau
Paris
◁

▷
GUSTAVE MOREAU
France
Salomé
Watercolor
Musée Gustave Moreau
Paris

94

ABEL FAIVRE
France
Elegant Woman
phite and crayon
Musée
du Petit Palais
Paris

FRANZ NIKLAUS KÖNIG *Switzerland* Peasant House in the Canton of Bern
Watercolor   Kunstmuseum, Basel

98

JOSEF ANTON KOCH *Germany* The Waterfall at Schmadribach
Watercolor Kunstmuseum, Basel

WILHELM LEIBL *Germany* Seated Man Smoking a Pipe
Pencil Staatliche Graphische Sammlung, Munich

Domenico Ranzoni *Italy* The Princess Saint-Léger on a Couch
Watercolor Collection Carlo Grassi, Galleria d'Arte Moderna, Milan

102

GIOVANNI SEGANTINI *Italy* Landscape with Figures
Crayon Collection Carlo Grassi, Galleria d'Arte Moderna, Milan

GAETANO PREVIATI *Italy* Peace
Pastel on canvas Collection Gaspare Gussoni, Milan

FRANÇOIS-MARIUS GRANET *France* Group of Figures
Sepia, wash, watercolor Collection R. R., Paris

104

the poet's portrait of Guys. The author of the *Fleurs du Mal* was here alluding to those innumerable flowers of flesh that bloom in Guys's ink drawings: proud horsewomen, pretty dancers, women of easy virtue and completely obvious charms. He loved horses and carriages, imperial festivals and military parades, but what he particularly observed, and always with a passionate eye, were women of all strata of society, whose characters he could capture in a few quick lines, whether they were princesses or prostitutes.

AN INSPIRED AMATEUR

The case of Constantin Guys, whose basic medium of expression was ink, is not unique in the nineteenth century. Another man was to exploit the resources of this technique and discover in it a surprising aspect of his creative genius: Victor Hugo (page 59, 86).

Few other works have such a great ability, in such a fascinating way, to invite

ILYA YEFIMOVICH REPIN *Russia* Portrait of Eleonora Duse Charcoal on canvas Tretyakov Art Gallery, Moscow

GUSTAVE COURBET *France* Portrait of the Artist (The Man with the Pipe)
Charcoal Wadsworth Atheneum, Hartford, Connecticut

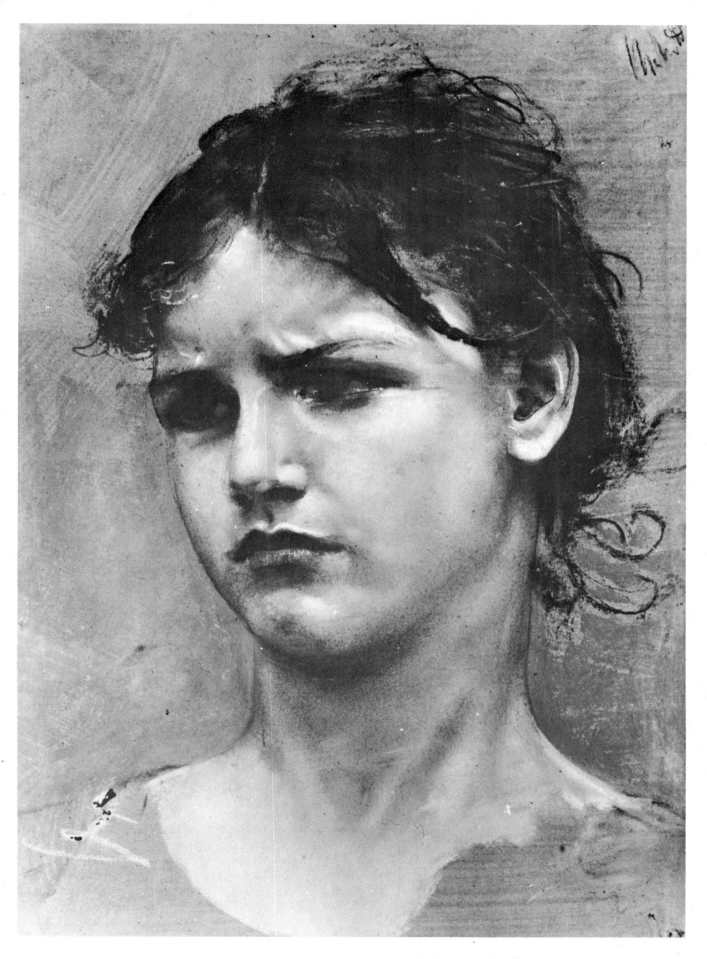

FRANCESCO MICHETTI *Italy* Head of a Young Girl
Charcoal Galleria Nazionale d'Arte Moderna, Rome

ODILON REDON *France* The Man with the Big Hat
Graphite Cabinet des Dessins, Louvre, Paris

study, as the drawings of Victor Hugo. After we have experienced their esthetic seduction and succumbed to the enchantment of a very mysterious quality that is found in the opacity of their shadows and in the strange whiteness of their light,

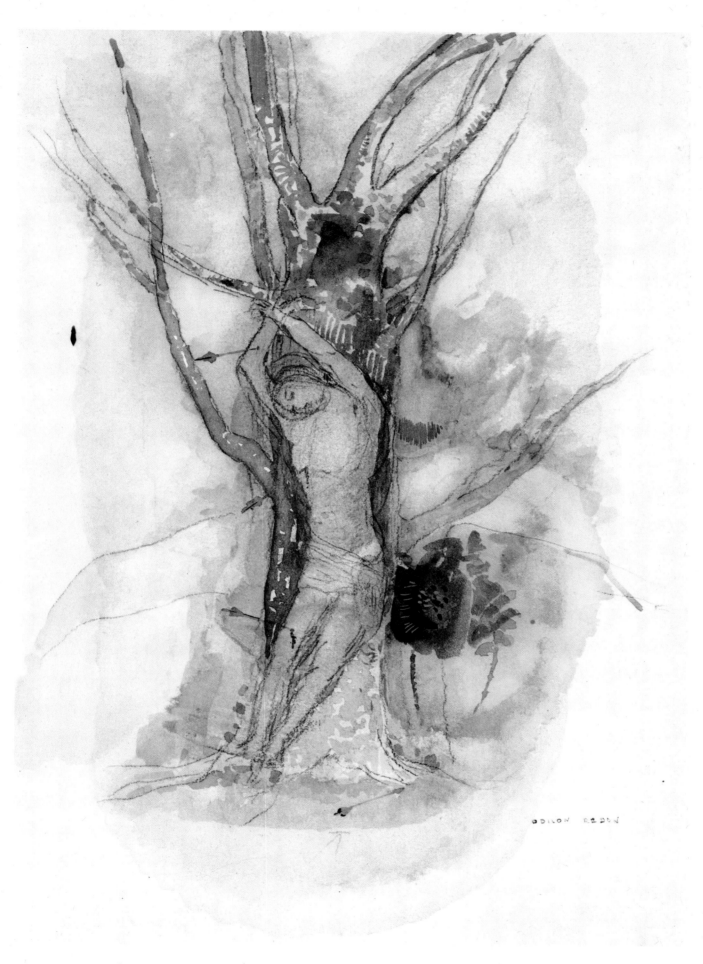

ODILON REDON *France* Saint Sebastian Oil on canvas Kunstmuseum, Basel 109

ODILON REDON *France* Closed Eyes
Red chalk Collection F., Paris

ODILON REDON *France* Music
Charcoal Private collection, Paris ▷

110

III

JOHAN BARTHOLD JONGKIND *Netherlands* Windmills
Watercolor Fogg Art Museum, Harvard University, Cambridge, Massachusetts

we are tempted to delve more deeply into the content of their themes, to discover the reasons for their repetition and to penetrate, by analysis, the significance of their formal components. Actually, we would like to turn to psychoanalysis in an attempt to discover an answer to everything in his pictures that poses us with an enigma and invites our examination.

If we attempt to understand the source of this power of suggestion possessed by a man who was in no way a professional practitioner of plastic expression, it seems that such a power is explained precisely by the fact that he was not a painter, that he expected nothing from his drawing, that his career and the essential area of his activity lay elsewhere, and that drawing could thus be the act by which he liberated himself from his literary preoccupations while abandoning himself to the pleasure of expressing something within him that did not have to be justified by words, and in a form that was all the more free since it in no way involved his artistic destiny.

But it would be dangerous to claim that he was thereby following a path that was opposed or foreign to his writing. A man like Hugo, powerfully charged with a system of thought that achieved a harmonious unity in his beliefs, his ideals, and even his contradictions, could not pursue different goals. It even appears that the true unity of his spirit, and his deepest personality, can be understood only by taking into consideration the part played by his drawing in his creative activity. This form of expression complemented the other. Through drawing, that role of the unspeakable, that opening into the obscure inner region of the individual, and those fantasies of uncontrolled dreams that in truth were always lacking in his poetic work, took concrete form.

For this reason the work of Victor Hugo as an artist should not be reduced to the status of a secondary occupation, like the violin for Ingres or drawing for Paul Valéry. On the contrary, for him it was undoubtedly an imperious passion, a necessity that endured for his entire life. If we nevertheless insist on regarding him as an amateur, we must admit that he was an inspired amateur. Even when his life was buffeted by hardships of all kinds, by dramas and sorrows, he spilled out his most ambitious dreams or his most tormented nightmares onto sheets of white paper, in more or less symbolic forms poured out in black ink. Speaking about a drawing that dates from 1856, that is, from his exile on Guernsey, he writes:

"On the other side of this page I have scribbled my own destiny: a ship, beaten by the tempest, in the middle of the monstrous ocean, practically lost, assailed by every hurricane and every wave, its only possession a little wisp of smoke called glory, which is whipped away by the wind — and which is its strength."

A school notebook shows that in 1817, when Hugo was fifteen, his notes for a history course were mingled with drawings done by an already skillful hand. This was a gift that he cultivated by himself, without any training other than his inclination toward pictorial representation of the objects that caught his attention, whether in his daily life, and especially during his travels, or in the imaginary world of his musings as a poet and novelist. Nevertheless, certain subjects that were to reappear under his pen with a strange persistence gradually imposed themselves upon him. It was only after long practice on detailed pencil drawings that he found his personal technique of India ink and sepia, to which he brought an increasingly powerful mastery, and remained faithful until the end of his life.

WILHELM LEIBL *Germany* Seated Man with Hat, Filling his Pipe
Pen drawing, Indian ink Staatliche Graphische Sammlung, Munich

FRANZ VON LENBACH *Germany* Peasant (Possibly Self-Portrait)
Pen drawing Staatliche Graphische Sammlung, Munich

LA MOLETTA

HENRI FANTIN-LATOUR *France* Self-Portrait
Graphite Former Collection Majowsky, Museum of Fine Arts, Budapest

Hugo probably amused himself on occasions with haphazard doodling, transforming inkblots, whose symmetry he obtained by folding the sheet of paper into four, into heraldic crests or other strange figures by means of a little retouching. But the patient, careful manner in which certain complicated architectural constructions are detailed, with pen or graphite, and the work required by his large wash landscapes (*Le Burg à la croix* — The Fortress of the Cross, which is admittedly the largest one, measures approximately 27″ by 48″), prove that despite the strenuous work involved in writing his books, he often spent long hours on the execution of a drawing.

Most of Victor Hugo's drawings (as well as his manuscripts) are kept in the Bibliothèque Nationale in Paris, and in his house in the Place des Vosges, where more than 350 of them can be seen. There are also some at Hauteville House, where he lived in Guernsey, and in the small museum that was formerly the Maison Vacquerie, at Villequier (Seine-Maritime).

Architecture in various forms is the dominant theme of this black-and-white imagery, where for some forty years it appeared with obsessive frequency. While we occasionally see trees and strange flowers, vegetation is rather rare in the Hugolian vision of landscape. His albums of drawings, the illustrated notes of his travels in Alsace, Switzerland, along the banks of the Rhine, and in Spain, his beautiful wash drawings of Guernsey and Luxembourg, reveal the important place occupied in his drawings by German castles, feudal towers, oriental palaces, castles of all kinds, Gothic cathedrals and chapels, belfries, old gabled and half-timbered houses, hilltop cities, fortifications, roofs bristling with spires and pinnacles, lighthouses, bridges, gates, stairways, fireplaces, and wayside Calvaries. Everything which the hand of man has constructed by assembling stones is there, worn by time and yet solid, suggesting the idea of a proud will when the edifice rises, as is frequently the case, on the peak of a mountain, into which it blends. Skies black with storm envelope romantic castles with the promise of a tempest, while a moonlit clarity bathes their walls, which seem to emerge from the depths of the darkest legend of the centuries.

While these architectural structures suggest the literary achievement that Victor Hugo constructed, with determination and courage, and while enduring the harshest blows of fate, in the face of wind and tide, they also appear as a symbol of his solitude. For these castles, citadels, and towers are often lost in the dunes, isolated in the middle of a desert — powerful, sad images to which correspond, here a tree planted in a vast, uncultivated field, there a boat scudding alone over the sea. Moreover, did not he himself stress this identification of his person with these monuments erected in inhuman landscapes? More than once his hand traced his name in letters that have the bulk of stones and that are arranged on the ground around an old castle.

During his long years on Guernsey, themes inspired by the sea appear frequently in his drawings: boats, cliffs, storms, shipwrecks, or simple movements of the waves, for which he discovered an admirable linear technique. Fairly detailed sketches are scattered through his writings, notes, and letters. Of all his manuscripts, the one that contains the largest number of, and the most important, illustrations is that of *Les Travailleurs de la mer* (Toilers of the Sea), whether the image is presented as a reflection of the written work or precedes the latter by recording on the paper what

ANSELM FEUERBACH *Germany* A Roman Woman
Charcoal Kupferstichkabinett, Basel

HONORÉ DAUMIER *France* Death and the Two Doctors
Watercolor and graphite Collection Oscar Reinhart, Winterthur

EUGÈNE BOUDIN *France* A Market in the Village Square
Watercolor Cabinet des Dessins, Louvre, Paris

HENRI HARPIGNIES *France* The Boulevard Saint-Germain
Watercolor Musée du Petit Palais, Paris

127

128

EDOUARD MANET *France* Portrait of Berthe Morisot Watercolor Private collection

ÉDOUARD MANET
France
The Model
at the Bar of
Folies Bergères
Pastel
Dijon Museum
Dijon

EDOUARD MANET *France* Olympia Watercolor and graphite Collection Stavros Niarchos

won by the French Revolution. The humorous drawing also led to the creation of a formula destined to enjoy a success that has been increasing right down to our own day — the picture story.

A BREATH OF HUMOR

The first in this line of picture-story artists was Rodolphe Töpffer, of Geneva (1799-1846). His drawings, which resembled quick sketches, were accompanied by a text in a cursive handwriting, the imaginativeness of which was full of droll humor. Between 1827 and 1844, Töpffer, who had also acquired a reputation as a writer with his *Nouvelles genevoises* (Geneva Tales), composed seven picture stories: *L'Histoire de Monsieur Vieux Bois, Voyages et aventures du docteur Festus, Monsieur Cryptogame, Monsieur Jabot, Monsieur Pencil, Monsieur Crépin*, and *L'Histoire de Jacques*. The heroes of other unfinished stories were named Cigare, Vertpré, and Tric-Trac.

Slightly later, in Germany, the best known of the picture-story artists was Wilhelm Busch (1832-1908), the author of the adventures of *Max und Moritz*, with its sometimes rather savage, very personal humor. At the same period in France, the important firm of Plon was publishing the humorous albums of Caran d'Ache (1858-1909): *Les Joies du plein air* (The Joys of the Open Air), *Le Prince Kozakokoff, À la découverte de la Russie* (On the Discovery of Russia), and others. The artist's real name was Emmanuel Poiré; a Russian, born in Moscow, he had taken his pseudonym from the Russian word for pencil, *karandash*. A collaborator on *La Vie Parisienne, Le Rire, La Vie Militaire*, and *La Caricature*, he also designed for the Théâtre d'Ombres du Chat-Noir the cardboard cutout figures for a show about the Napoleonic Era, the success of which drew crowds every evening to this Montmartre cabaret. Finally, at the close of the century, a new name appeared that was actually less well known than those of the heroes, so beloved of children, whom he created: Christophe (Georges Colomb), author of *La Famille Fenouillard* (1889), *Les Facéties du Sapeur Camember* (The Pranks of Sapper Camember) (1890), and *L'Idée Fixe du savant Cossinus* (The Obsession of Cossinus the Scholar) (1893).

While there was a certain relationship and affiliation between these narrative pictures and popular imagery, which also told stories, their spirit was entirely different. Töpffer, Busch, Caran d'Ache, and Christophe were highly skilled artists, and the fact that they sometimes expressed themselves through simple methods that might cause them to pass for unsophisticated or unskilled was simply an added attraction. The naïveté and crudeness of the popular artists were not feigned, and if the lack of skill of the drawings they engraved on wood added to their charm, it was precisely because it formed a natural complement to the freshness of their imagination. These artists took their subjects from history and legend, using stories of kings, fairies, and saints, without neglecting current events, which were always rich in those "shocking dramas" and "extraordinary adventures" that the artists fed into their "penny dreadfuls," that early form of the picture newspaper.

Aside from a few names, such as that of François Georgin (1801-1863), who for a long time worked for Épinal, drawing the entire series of illustrations of Napo-

BERTHE MORISOT *France* Study of Girls Sewing
Red chalk Musée du Petit Palais, Paris

BERTHE MORISOT *France* The Dancer
Drawing Collection Albert Pasche, Geneva ▷

Berthe Morisot

EDOUARD MANET *France* La Toilette
Red chalk Former Collection Marcel Guérin, Paris

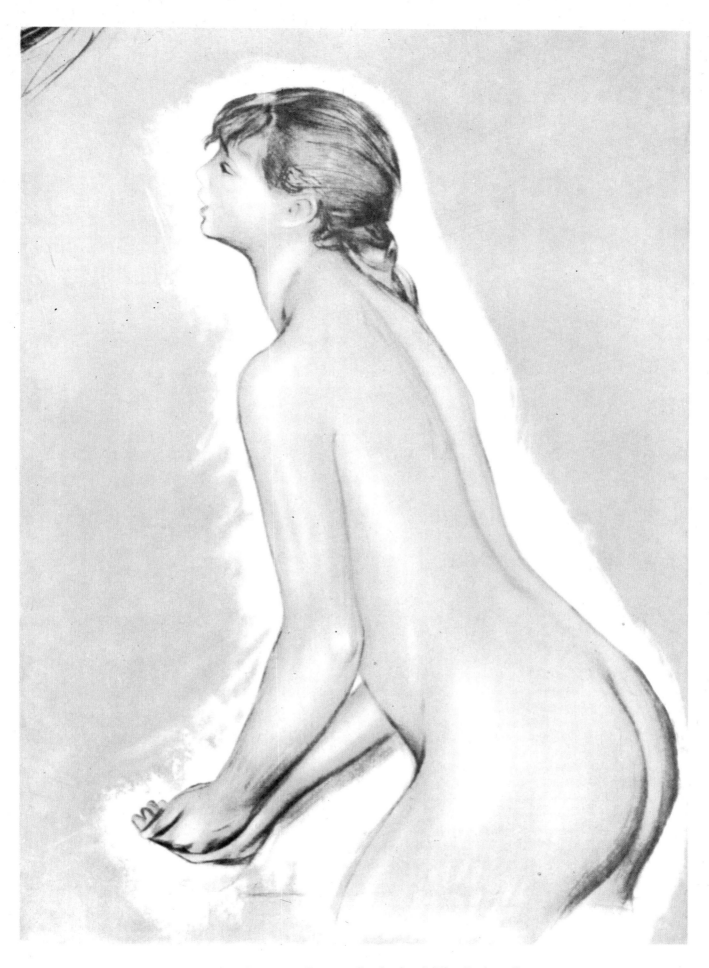

Auguste Renoir *France* Study for " The Bathers "
Colored chalk Art Institute of Chicago

AUGUSTE RENOIR *France* Coco Painting
Red chalk Private Collection

AUGUSTE RENOIR *France* Laundresses
Red chalk and graphite Private collection

AUGUSTE RENOIR *France* Study of Nude
Graphite and gouache Cabinet des Dessins, Louvre, Paris

EDOUARD MANET *France* Study for " La Toilette "
Red chalk Courtauld Institute, London

142

AUGUSTE RENOIR *France* Two Women on a Red Ground
Pastel   Rudolf Staechelin-Familienstiftung, Basel

AUGUSTE RENOIR *France* Jean Renoir with a Hat
Pastel   National Museum, Belgrade

EDOUARD MANET *France* Study of Female Nude
Graphite and chalk on tinted paper Private Collection

AUGUSTE RENOIR *France* Portrait of Berthe Morisot and Her Daughter
Pastel Musée du Petit Palais, Paris

Camille Pissarro *France* Landscape at Eragny
Watercolor   Collection Albert Pasche, Geneva

PAUL CÉZANNE *France* Still Life with Inkwell
Watercolor Collection Mr. and Mrs. Paul M. Hirschland, New York

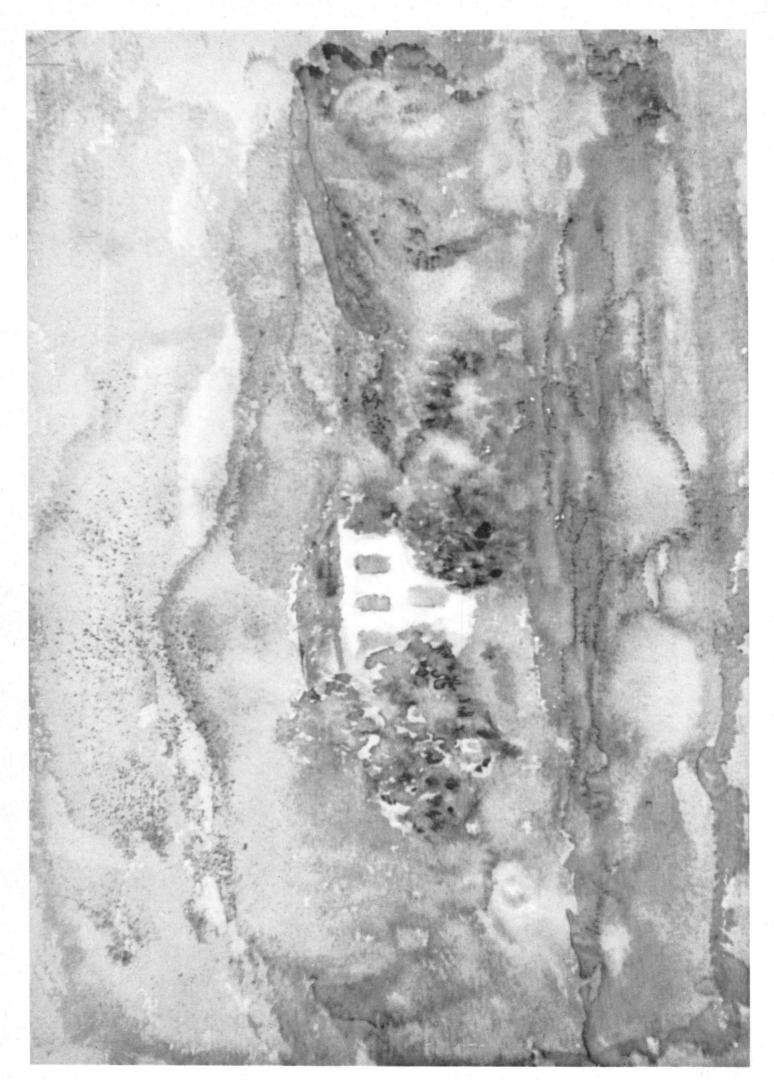

AUGUSTE RENOIR *France* House Hidden Among Trees, Cagnes Watercolor Musée du Petit Palais, Paris

CLAUDE MONET *France* Dutch Seascape   Collection Durand-Ruel, Paris

ALFRED SISLEY *France* Early Snowfall in a French Village
Pastel Former Collection Majowsky, Museum of Fine Arts, Budapest

CLAUDE MONET *France* Waterloo Bridge, London Pastel Cabinet des Dessins, Louvre, Paris

leon's major battles, almost all of these artists are unknown to us. Nevertheless, it would have been unjust to omit mention of the grace and savor of their work, which assures them a special place in the history of drawing in the nineteenth century.

For the same reason we shall mention the authors, most of them anonymous, of those romantic, naïve gouaches that were very popular in Italy between 1830 and 1850 and that depict views of Vesuvius erupting. These landscapists, most of them Neapolitan, belonged to what was called the *Piccola Scuola di Posillipo* (Little School of Posillipo). They occasionally added to these pictures of the famous bay and the famous crater a realistic image of a beautiful boat or the ruins of Herculaneum, preferably seen by moonlight.

When we add to these categories of artists those who were painters or pastel artists in their spare time, and who made a name for themselves by publishing drawings in newspapers, we realize what a prodigious diversity of techniques and styles went to form the work of the artists of this century that was so rich in trailblazing achievements. Among these artists were Jean-Louis Forain (page 124), whose biting spirit and implacable pencil contributed to the success of *Le Journal* and *Le Figaro;* Théodore Steinlen (page 209), an inhabitant of Montmartre, of Swiss origin, an observer of the vagabonds and the poor, the illustrator of Jehan Rictus, a poster painter, and a collaborator on the *Chat-Noir*, *Gil Blas*, and *L'Assiette au beurre;* and Abel Faivre, whose frivolous or savage drawings appeared in *Le Rire*, *Le Journal*, and *L'Echo de Paris* (page 97).

IDEALISTS AND SYMBOLISTS

It is above all by form — that is, by drawing — that painting signals, in the course of its history, its changes of orientation. In most cases a painter's drawings provide us with a definition of his esthetics and a schematic interpretation of the school to which he belongs.

This was the case with the Pre-Raphaelites, whose drawings reveal, in even more detailed fashion than their paintings, their astonishing purpose: to return, in the middle of the nineteenth century, to an esthetics that antedated that of Raphael. They failed in their purpose, and the most that can be seen in their works is the reappearance of a mannerism that relates them more closely to a decadent school of the Renaissance than to medieval painting. Moreover, the ideas of John Ruskin, which were the source of this movement, were interpreted in various ways by the painters of the group, who were united, by way of a great deal of mysticism and much literature by their fondness for allegory and symbol. In this they resembled a group of German painters who had earlier made a name for themselves in Rome as the "Nazarenes," a group that included Johann Friedrich Overbeck, Schnorr von Carolsfeld, Joseph Anton Koch, and others.

Comparing the dates, it is amusing to note that at the same period when Gustave Courbet in France was founding the realist school and anathematizing everything in painting that was not "representation of visible and tangible objects," in England the Pre-Raphaelite Brotherhood was developing exactly the opposite theory. Its principal representatives, Sir John Everett Millais, William Holman

EDGAR DEGAS *France* Mademoiselle Salle
Pastel Collection Countess Jean de Polignac

PAUL CÉZANNE *France* Flowerpots
Watercolor Cabinet des Dessins, Louvre, Paris

158

PAUL CÉZANNE *France* The Sainte Victoire Mountain
Watercolor Private collection, Paris

EDGAR DEGAS *France* Dancer Tying Her Slipper Pastel Collection Durand-Ruel, Paris and New York

Hunt, and particularly Sir Edward Coley Burne-Jones (page 69) and Dante Gabriel Rossetti (page 68), have left drawings in which the very exaggeration of the stylistic effort to express the intensity and purity of certain emotions, the impulses of the heart and of faith, and the "torments of the soul," was translated into an indisputably baroque esthetics which did, however, evince genuine loftiness of soul. In the worst cases this esthetics is much more bearable in black and white than in color. Certain portraits, with their somewhat supernatural and spectral character, also have a kind of nobility and charm, like Rossetti's portrait of his future wife, Elizabeth Siddal (Victoria and Albert Museum).

Strangely enough, these dreams of a return to Gothic painting bore fruit in the creation of the Art Nouveau style. But before the latter had completely taken shape and appeared in the work of artists of whom we shall later have occasion to speak, the idealistic current, propagated in England by the Pre-Raphaelites, appeared in other forms in other countries: in Germany with Hans von Marées (page 233), in Switzerland with Arnold Böcklin (page 73), and in France with Puvis de Chavannes (pages 57, 58) and Gustave Moreau (pages 94, 95).

The symbolist language with which Moreau attempted to express himself in painting involved him in compositions whose theoretical ambitions were not always buttressed by solid pictorial qualities. But what particularly interests us in his work are his watercolors, to which he brought a freedom of vision and technique not found in his paintings. He is, in fact, a striking example of the divergence between two styles of expression that may be created in an artist's work by the use of two such dissimilar techniques. Gustave Moreau was a draftsman with the precision of a jeweler. Even in his large canvases the refinement and proliferation of details often take on the character of an overelaborate, hallucinated diligence. We realize the work involved in the preparation of his canvases when we look at the innumerable pencil and ink studies in which he sought gradually to elaborate the style of his more or less imaginary figures. From an unfinished, partially painted canvas entitled *Poétesses indiennes*, we also learn how the final drawing, in which nothing was neglected or left to improvisation, took shape on the white canvas. This canvas, one of his best compositions, which represents five women grouped on an intricate rock form at the edge of a luminous body of water, is today in the Musée Gustave Moreau, together with 350 watercolors and more than 7,000 drawings.

This meticulous construction, which the artist used as a foundation for painting his pictures, is completely absent from his watercolors, in which the brush, laden with color, seems to have spontaneously and directly outlined figures and landscapes on the paper, without any preliminary drawing. The forms become so free and light that this mythical universe, from which emerge Orpheus, Galatea, Delilah, Salome, and their inseparable cortege of sphinxes, griffons, chimeras, and unicorns, disintegrates into a *tachisme* that is close to abstraction.

The work of every nineteenth-century painter includes watercolors that represent for the individual artist a special way of expressing his sensibility. It is possible that without the watercolor the personalities of Turner, Barye, Delacroix, Bonington, Jongkind, and Boudin might never have been completely revealed. Without the watercolor, Gustave Moreau might never have discovered that passage through which his work made major advances along a road that leads directly into the twentieth century.

PAUL CÉZANNE *France* Portrait of Achille Empereire
Charcoal Kupferstichkabinett, Basel

PAUL CÉZANNE *France* Profile of a Man
Pencil   Kupferstichkabinett, Basel

Still others asserted a major part of their creative faculties through the watercolor. Cézanne (pages 151, 158, 159, 162, 163, 169, 185) discovered in the watercolor a perfect medium for the formulation of an esthetics of fragmentation in which, through a slow explosion of forms that are thenceforth suggested only by planes of color scattered throughout the landscape, both light and air seem to circulate in a space rendered almost tangible by the white of the paper.

For Berthe Morisot (pages 134, 135), who was weaned away from Corot's influence by that of Manet, and who developed the most brilliant (but not the most disciplined) side of his painting until it became her own style, the watercolor was often her most successful medium for the expression of her conception of impressionism. She brought to it that extreme mobility of stroke that watercolor painting seems to render more sensitive and spontaneous. The catalogue (prefaced by Paul Valéry) of an exhibition of her works at the Galerie Dru in 1926 mentions forty watercolors, indicating that she did not stop practicing this technique, together with those of the pastel and the crayon, until 1894, that is, until a year before her death.

Finally, Rodin (pages 202, 203) discovered in the fluidity of watercolor a method of depicting the feminine body that was divorced from the violence and tortured spirit of his sculpture, and the admirable work inspired by this medium is of a more delicate but no less quivering sensuality and a great linear purity.

THE REHABILITATION OF THE PASTEL

It would be impossible to discover a similar interest in pastel, for artists had shown little inclination, for quite some time, to experiment with its resources. No particularly interesting work in this medium appeared before the end of the century, but several names then appeared to compensate for this persistent eclipse, and the pastel suddenly acquired a brilliance and expressive power it had never before achieved, not even among the great pastel artists of the eighteenth century.

The period from 1870 to 1900 begins and ends with the work of two great artists to whom we owe this renaissance of the pastel, and who used it in completely different ways: Edgar Degas (pages 157, 160, 165, 166, 167, 168, 170, 171) and Odilon Redon. Degas at first utilized it for portraits and landscapes, although the landscape had interested him only briefly (for instance very beautiful seascapes that date from 1869). But beginning in 1875, he adopted pastel as his preferred medium, and gradually this preference almost completely supplanted oil painting. Two reasons can be advanced for this choice. First, Degas was a very great draftsman; his painting is founded on a profound knowledge and understanding of drawing, and the pastel is, physically speaking, a draftsman's medium. The second reason explains his continued use of pastel: when his eyesight began to weaken, long before almost total blindness set in, and when for this reason (especially after 1885) he was forced to replace the pencil by charcoal for the execution of his drawings, because of its heavier and darker line, the pastel, which required similar treatment, harmonized perfectly with charcoal work. From then on, his major works were executed in pastel, and he experimented with all possible methods (including several of his own invention that we shall study later) of utilizing it with new effectiveness.

EDGAR DEGAS *France* Julie Belleli
Tempera Dumbarton Oaks Research Library and Collection

EDGAR DEGAS *France* Woman Ironing
Pastel and white chalk   Louvre, Paris

Edgar Degas *France* Study of a Violinist
Pastel and charcoal The Metropolitan Museum of Art, New York

EDGAR DEGAS *France* Dancers at the Ballet-Bar
Pastel   Duncan Phillips Memorial Gallery, Washington, D.C.

PAUL GAUGUIN *France* Study of a Breton Peasant Woman
Charcoal and pastel Cabinet des Dessins, Louvre, Paris

173

ALFRED SISLEY *France* Head of a Young Boy
Graphite Cabinet des Dessins, Louvre, Paris

PAUL GAUGUIN *France* Breton Dance Pastel Stedelijk Museum, Amsterdam

ARMAND GUILLAUMIN *France* Pile of Sand on the Bank of the Seine Pastel Musée du Petit Palais, Paris

PAUL GAUGUIN   *France*   "Te Arii Vahine" (Beauty Queen)   Watercolor   Collection Ward Cheney, New York

PAUL GAUGUIN *France* Tahitian Woman
Watercolor   Grenoble Museum, Grenoble

VINCENT VAN GOGH *Holland* Washerwomen
India ink, reed pen Kröller-Müller Museum, Otterlo

He even pulverized sticks of pastel and added water to the powder, applying the resulting product with a brush.

For Degas the background of a work was the object of studies and experiments that led him into strange innovations. Thus he utilized monotypes as foundations for pastels. We have seen the remarkable results he obtained from a method that in his hands achieved such an unusual character that some of these monotypes, particularly the landscapes, seem almost like abstract works. For his pastels he used the weakest of several proofs obtained with the metal plate, on which he had painted directly with oil or varnish. The pastel drawing was done on the proof when it was dry, with very beautiful results. In this manner Degas composed, between 1876 and 1879, *Le Café-concert " Les Ambassadeurs"* (Musée de Lyon), *Le Duo* (Robert von Hirsch Collection, Basel), *Trois filles assises* — Three Girls Seated (Maurice Exsteens Collection, Le Vésinet), and *Femmes à la terrasse* — Ladies on the Terrace (Musée des Impressionnistes, Paris). Sometimes he used a lithograph rather than a

VINCENT VAN GOGH *Holland* Garden with Peasant Woman and Hen
Watercolor, gouache. graphite Vincent Van Gogh Foundation, Amsterdam

VINCENT VAN GOGH *Holland* Orchard in Provence
India ink, reed pen; touches of white Vincent Van Gogh Foundation, Amsterdam

monotype for his base, as in the pastel of *Femme sortant du bain* — Woman Emerging from the Bath (Louvre), done in 1877.

Even when he employed the pastel alone on paper or, preferably, on cardboard, as in *Le Tub* (1886) or *Après le bain, femme s'essuyant le cou* — Woman Drying Her Neck After a Bath (1898), both in the Louvre, the various techniques combined in superimposed layers — misty, blended tones for the background, and a graphic texture obtained by juxtaposed lines or hatchings, for the principal figures — gave the work, through the blending of velvety shadows and very clear lights, that depth of space and vigor of relief so characteristic of Degas's pastels. He also did numerous brush drawings with varnish on cardboard, a method of expression particularly favored by Toulouse-Lautrec.

Unlike the pastel artists of an earlier age, Degas never considered the pastel as particularly intended for the expression of the charm of an atmosphere or the tenderness of a feminine face. He endowed it with an energy until then unknown. The same cannot be said of Manet (pages 128, 129, 130, 131, 132, 136, 141, 144,

183

VINCENT VAN GOGH *Holland* View of an Industrial City Collection U. W. W. Van Gogh, Stedelijk Museum, Amsterdam

PAUL CÉZANNE *France* House in Provence Watercolor Collection Mr. and Mrs. F. H. Hirschland, New York

ARMAND GUILLAUMIN *France* Portrait of a Young Girl Pastel Private collection

PAUL GAUGUIN *France* Portrait of a Woman
Charcoal and pastel Collection Mme. Dina Vierny, Paris

PAUL GAUGUIN *France* Tahitian Woman
Pastel The Brooklyn Museum, Brooklyn, New York

188

Henri de Toulouse-Lautrec *France* The English Girl at the Star Cabaret, Le Havre
Red chalk with touches of white Albi Museum, Albi

193

of the extent to which the history of drawing diverged from the history of painting during the nineteenth century (pages 108, 109, 110, 111).

Although he had studied painting, and although portraits, flowers, and landscapes appeared from time to time, on a small scale, in his work, for almost twenty years Redon found in drawing the only completely satisfying method of expression. For him, charcoal possessed inexhaustible resources; this was later to become true of lithography as well, to which he had been initiated in his youth in Bordeaux, by the engraver Rodolphe Bresdin (page 85).

Bresdin himself was an artist with a very unusual personality. Any subject was for him a pretext for the depiction of a luxuriant, intricate vegetal world, abounding in mysterious details in which the eye loses itself in a tangle of branches, grasses, and vines, among which some vaguely animal form or undefined skeleton always seems to be concealed. The drawing pen which he also used for his lithographs, gave a disturbing quality of precision to his visionary landscapes.

Redon always retained for Bresdin the admiration a disciple feels for a teacher whose instruction has been of value to him. He did indeed learn much from Bresdin. Redon's drawings, however, are situated in a completely different universe, although it is composed in similar fashion of a combination of the real and the imaginary. The approximately 500 charcoal drawings he left are not simple studies or sketches, but elaborate compositions that form a fundamental creative work in his life.

In these charcoal drawings Redon became the interpreter of what he called "the obscure world of the indefinite," a world that resembles those dreams in which the intensity of certain impressions causes us to doubt their unreal quality, and which are experienced as images of an agonizing reality. For in the ambiguity that tinges all these semifantastic beings who emerge from skillful chiaroscuro effects, a given detail suggests the observation of a natural phenomenon rather than the vision of an imaginary scene. Something disturbing is born of this ambiguity, of which Redon developed more than one poetic and dramatic aspect in the series of lithographs that he began in 1878, on themes inspired by Edgar Poe, Gustave Flaubert, and St. John's Apocalypse.

But this mysterious content of Redon's drawings, and those often monstrous creatures that seem to be looking at us with the icy irony of his *Araignée souriante* (The Grinning Spider) or the terrible eye of his *Cyclopes* were to disappear in the enchantments of color and light to which first pastel and then painting belatedly led him. He did not, however, renounce the esthetics of uncertainty that maintained his work to the very end in a domain continually divided between the real and the fabulous. Even the fascinating flowers with which he composed numerous pastel bouquets seem to have been picked, not from nature, but in a dream garden. The nightmare has given way to the pleasant dream, and in the serenity of an imagination delivered up to happiness but still fond of mystery, the aging artist created his *Chars d'Apollon* (Chariots of Apollo), haloed with sun, *Profils de Femme* (Profiles of Woman) emerging from heavens whose clouds are flowers, and shells from which radiant Venuses are born.

At the same time that the pastel was being rehabilitated, sanguine was regaining the long-lost favor in which it had formerly been held by artists. Redon made

HENRI DE TOULOUSE-LAUTREC *France* Head of a Madman Charcoal Albi Museum, Albi

HENRI DE TOULOUSE-LAUTREC *France* The Animal Trainer
Red chalk Albi Museum, Albi

beautiful use of it in such drawings as *Les Yeux clos* (The Closed Eyes) from the former Pontremoli Collection, reproduced here for the first time. This is a theme he depicted several times in paintings; there also exists a pastel version and a lithograph. Sometimes he combined sanguine with pastel, as in the portraits of Madame Redon (Louvre) and Marie Botkin (Arï Redon Collection), which demonstrate the penetrating manner in which the painter, whatever medium he was using, knew how to examine a face and translate all its depth of reflection or dreaminess.

Sanguine drawings exist in the work of all the artists who experimented extensively with the techniques of drawing and who, whether they were painters or sculptors, were passionately fond of drawing, including Renoir (pages 137, 138, 139, 140, 142, 143, 145, 146, 148, 149, 152, 191, 214), Berthe Morisot, Suzanne Valadon (pages 220, 221), and Maillol (pages 205, 208).

Aside from Degas and Cézanne, whom it is difficult to consider as impressionists although they participated in their exhibitions, it was Renoir in particular who, of all the impressionist painters, was a great draftsman. Monet (pages 153, 155), in his sketchbooks, landscapes done in pencil or black chalk, and sketches for paintings, undoubtedly executed interesting drawings, but we are obliged to admit that they are not as revelatory of his personality as his paintings. This was also true of Sisley (pages 154, 174) and Pissarro (pages 150, 172, 190). Impressionism implied attention predominantly paid to a certain moving aspect of color and to a vibration of light that was opposed to an exacting definition of forms. It could be a technique only of painting, not of drawing.

AN ARTIST IN BLACK AND WHITE

Drawing was, as a matter of fact, the method of reaction against impressionism chosen by those who, like Seurat (pages 212, 218, 219), reproached it for its lack of structure, its excessive softness, and the evanescence of what constituted its esthetics of retinal sensation.

However, it was on color and on the analysis of the phenomena of color perception that Seurat based the pictorial theory of divisionism. But its application required a strictly constructed drawing, since in such an intellectual style of painting nothing could be left to chance, improvisation, or the instinctive movements of the hand. Later, moreover, when he complemented his method of optical combination (or pointillism) with considerations directly inspired by the theories of Charles Henry on the emotional signification of lines, Seurat took these theories into consideration in the drawing of his last major works — *La Parade* (The Outside Show), *Le Chahut* (The Shindig), and *Le Cirque* (The Circus) — observing the laws of a genuine "scientific esthetic" in the ascending or descending movement of the structural lines of his compositions.

Thus his conception of drawing came to be more and more closely linked with his conception of color. It has nothing in common, however, with the pointillist technique, and this is why, despite the fact that in his drawings we find most of the themes he used in his painting, Seurat the draftsman was clearly distinct from

HENRI DE TOULOUSE-LAUTREC *France* Yvette Guilbert Bowing
Pencil and watercolor Providence, Rhode Island, Museum of Art, Rhode Island School of Design

HENRI DE TOULOUSE-LAUTREC *France* May Belfort
Oil on paper Gates Mills, Ohio, Collection Mr. and Mrs. Frank Kern Griesinger

HENRI DE TOULOUSE-LAUTREC *France* Oscar Wilde
Watercolor Collection Durand-Ruel, New York

Seurat the painter, and achieved in black and white a body of work the study of which is absolutely necessary for a complete understanding of his personality.

Like all cautious beginners Seurat began by drawing, with graphite and in a very academic fashion, nudes, plaster casts, and copies of the old masters. But he was interested, very early in his career, in all speculative thinking about art, and in all experiments that sought to codify methods of execution. He found a guide to the new methods, and encouragement for the ideas obsessing him, in a book that has now fallen into disuse but that in those days enjoyed a great reputation: Charles Blanc's *Grammaire des Arts du dessin* (Grammar of the Arts of Design), published in 1870. The author, a member of the Institut and a founder of the *Gazette des Beaux-Arts*, expressed his ideas in a picturesque style that sometimes brings a smile to the reader's face. "Drawing is the masculine sex of art; color is its feminine sex," he writes. Knowing the traditional superiority claimed by the stronger sex over the weaker, we are to conclude from this distinction that drawing is superior to painting, according to the old hierarchical classification of which we have already spoken. The author declares that drawing must maintain its preponderance, for otherwise painting would be lost through color "as humanity was lost through Eve."

Making allowance for the ridiculous aspect of this language, we can understand how Seurat found in Charles Blanc's book support for his desire to formulate rules that would reconcile his view with his desire for method. He was also able to find in it confirmation of the importance that he himself attached to drawing and that later sufficed to justify his estrangement from impressionism. As early as 1881, that is, even before he had discovered the very personal style that was to mark the advent of neoimpressionism in painting, Seurat had found the style of his drawings.

In 1883 — he was then twenty-four years of age and had only eight years ahead of him in which to achieve his work — his first submission accepted by the Salon was a drawing: the portrait of the painter Aman-Jean (today in the Metropolitan Museum in New York), done in Conté crayon in a technique to which he was to remain faithful until his death. In the same period his admiration for Millet was demonstrated not only by the priority — fundamental in his case, of secondary importance for Millet — given to shadows, but also by his choice of themes. *Paysans aux champs* (Peasants in the Fields), *Le Travail de la terre* (Work on the Soil), *Les Deux campagnards* (The Two Rustics), and *Le Labourage* (Plowing) are characteristic subjects of Seurat's early works, done in a style that he was soon to perfect and that would permit him to execute approximately 400 drawings.

Although some of his drawings — Parisian landscapes, pictures of dreary suburbs, cabs, locomotives—were completely unrelated to the themes of his painting, it was particularly the long and careful preparation of his large pictures that provided him with an opportunity to execute some very beautiful pencil sketches. Their role seems to have been to serve as experiments in black and white and in intermediate gray tonalities, for the values of the future coloring of a canvas. He was able to make a final choice, from among the variants of these sketches, of the most desirable juxtapositions of values, as in the groupings and isolated figures in *Un dimanche d'été à l'Ile de la Grande Jatte* (A Summer Sunday on the Isle of the Grande Jatte), which he began to paint only after he had executed thirty-one rough oil sketches and twenty-three drawings as studies for its various sections. A pencil sketch of the couple seen in

AUGUSTE RODIN *France* Meditation
Watercolor   Private collection, Paris

Auguste Rodin *France* The Woman and the Siren

Watercolor   Galerie Beyeler, Basel   203

the foreground, at the right of the composition, shows that the values of the color masses — the hats, clothing, and parasol — were determined in the drawing even before the silhouette of the couple had acquired its final form. Another drawing for the same painting shows a more developed version with the woman fishing, the construction and values of which are exactly the same ones that will be assigned to her in the completed picture.

All the figures, including the dogs and the monkey, of this large painting, whose charm is at once hieratic and popular, must also have been tested in black and white before being admitted to the canvas in color form. This procedure was followed by Seurat in every one of his works, and has given us several excellent drawings for *Les Poseuses* (The Models), *La Parade*, and *Le Chahut*. Looking at them, we are amazed that such depth could have been obtained in the shadows by the simple method of rubbing with a Conté crayon. In the lighter areas the grain of the paper remains visible, the modeling being suggested rather than clearly stated in the figures, in which a linear outline never appears. The same method, but sometimes with light touches of white gouache, was used for the execution of the drawings, done around 1888, in which the painter studied the atmosphere of a *café-concert* (nightclub); as in *La Parade* where we see, over the heads of the spectators, a singer on the stage of the Eden-Concert, the Gaîté Rochechouart, or the Européen.

Very rarely did Seurat attempt to reproduce in his drawings the pointillist technique of his paintings, as was sometimes done by other adepts of neoimpressionism — Pissarro (with crayon), Signac, and Dubois-Pillet. However, there exist studies in India ink and pen for *Les Poseuses* and *La Parade* in which Seurat patiently "pointillized" the figures and the background.

While working on the paintings of his last years, his drawing became increasingly sensitive to certain arabesque movements that were to characterize *Le Chahut*, the *Jeune femme se poudrant* (Young Woman Powdering Herself), and *Le Cirque* with the stamp of Art Nouveau: the spirit of the baroque of 1900 was already appearing in 1890. At the same time he was studying the principles of a graphical language that tended to give significance to the outline of every form. The last known drawing from his hand, a simple sketch of the clown seen from behind in the foreground of his last canvas, *le Cirque* (which death prevented him from finishing), defines the strange form, in three bristling locks, of the hair of this figure, on which the entire composition seems to rest. Seurat was careful to emphasize in a written note that for him this form, which simultaneously resembles a flower and a triple- or quadruple-tongued flame, was a symbol of joy. We find it in *La Parade*, in the guise of small flames bursting out along the row of lights at the top of the canvas. In the pen drawing, where almost everything is already in place for the painting, we notice that this form is not shown; thus it was not until later that the globes that are the source of this lighting were transformed into "symbols of joy." In *Le Chahut* the pointed, or cornute, flower appears in the ribbon bows on the dancers' shoulders and shoes, as it was later to appear as a wallpaper motif in the room in which the *Jeune femme se poudrant* is sitting. Lastly, *Le Cirque* seems to have been totally conceived under this sign, which appears in the painting some twenty times in various forms: in the hair and collar of the clown in the foreground, in the dress of the rider, in the mane and tail of the horse, the hands of the acrobat and the clown in the background, in various details of the spectators' clothing, and so on.

ARISTIDE MAILLOL *France* The Laundress Red chalk and pastel Collection Mme. Dina Vierny, Paris

ANTOINE-EMILE
BOURDELLE
France
Seated Man
Carbon pencil
Bourdelle Museum
Paris

As for the Art Nouveau style that prevails to a certain extent in all his work, it seems that Seurat owes it in large part to Jules Chéret, whom he admired, and whose charming posters adorned the walls of Paris. Moreover, the critics of the time did not fail to establish a relationship between the figures of Chéret and the dancers of *Le Chahut*.

WITH A STROKE OF THE BRUSH

Chéret, however, was not the only artist to capture in his drawing the graphic spirit that was flowering in a thousand different ways in the Art Nouveau style. He was the first to use color for posters, yet Toulouse-Lautrec obtained more striking effects in his lithographs. But it was only in 1891 (the year of Seurat's death) that Lautrec did his first poster for la Goulue. Like many painters of the time, he had gone through a "Japanese crisis," of which more than one trace can be seen in his conception of composition. The relationships between Japanese drawings and the style of 1900 have not as yet been sufficiently explored, but they are obvious. Lautrec's personality was, however, much too strong not to dominate every influence and transform it into a component of his own individual style (pages 193, 195, 196, 198, 199, 200, 217).

He was above all else a draftsman, and we may even say that he was a draftsman in his painting; in his canvases the color is frequently laid on in long strokes and hatchings, as if he were using a pencil. Moreover, he reduced painting and drawing to a single technique, for a great number of his works, including some of his best, are drawings done on cardboard with the end of the brush and with paint greatly diluted with varnish. The *Femme qui tire son bas* (Woman Pulling on Her Stocking — Musée d'Albi), which dates from 1894, is a beautiful example of this method. Sometimes, as in two works of 1892 — the *Femme au boa noir* (Woman in a Black Boa) and *Jane Avril dansant* (Jane Avril Dancing), both in the Louvre — only the faces were painted with a certain attention to the modeling, while the background and dresses were handled in a graphic manner that permitted the cardboard to be seen between the long strokes of the brush. Unlike Degas, Lautrec was little interested in the pastel, although we do possess certain drawings in which he made use of this medium, among others the *Portrait de Van Gogh* of 1887.

Lautrec had been conquered by a passion for drawing at a very early age, and his school notebooks were full of pen sketches. Those sketches still in existence, which date from around 1878, when he was not yet fifteen, already reveal an astonishing sureness of line. His skill in capturing the movements of a horse predisposed him for the numerous drawings he was later to make of the riders of the Cirque Fernando and jockeys on their mounts. During his stay at the Maison de Santé in Neuilly in 1899, where he underwent treatment for his alcoholism, he drew from memory thirty-nine circus drawings in crayon, twenty-two of which were published in a facsimile album four years after his death, in 1905. Some of these drawings, like *La Clownesse sur un cheval blanc* (The Lady Clown on a White Horse), which depicts the kneeling movement of a horse bowing, are typical of the extraordinary ease with which Lautrec could handle the most difficult subjects.

PIERRE LAPRADE
France
Landscape
Watercolor
Collection R. R.
Paris

211

GEORGES SEURAT *France* Plowing Conté crayon Cabinet des Dessins, Louvre, Paris

His youthful drawings, however, are not always accurate auguries of the audacious and spirited style of his maturity, of which his posters offer a perfect synthesis. But beginning in 1882, his eighteenth year, his charcoal drawings of his mother, the Countess Adèle de Toulouse-Lautrec Monfa, although still stamped with a certain classical austerity, nevertheless reveal a precision and vigor that pose a challenge to the remark made by Léon Bonnat (whose studio he entered that same year): "Your drawing is terrible."

Lautrec's great period is that of his life in Montmartre, the period of balls, bars, cabarets, and brothels. The vision of these agitated evenings and questionable nights, and his ability to observe with a penetrating and often implacable eye the singers, dancers, and prostitutes of the Mirliton, the Moulin de la Galette, the Moulin Rouge and the Divan Japonais, have given us these drawings that are superb documents of a certain aspect of Paris at the turn of the century. They are the brilliant expression of the frenzy of living in which the little crippled man buried his human melancholy in the combination of art and pleasure.

The charcoal studies enhanced with color, and the brush drawings he did in preparation for the composition of his posters, are among his most interesting works; in them he seems to have gone as far as possible in his search for a formula that would be at once expressive and synthetical. They contain fascinating portraits: the monochrome sketch of the singer Caudieux, whose rolling gait and frock coat with flapping tails remind us of Georgius; Yvette Guilbert, whom Lautrec did not hesitate to depict in caricatural form, to the great displeasure of the singer, who did not want this drawing for her poster; the Irish girl May Belfort, of whom he did several paintings and lithographs, and whom he depicted with the little black cat she held in her arms while singing on the stage of the "Décadents" nightclub, "I've got a little cat — I'm very fond of that..."; Missia Natanson, whom he drew in black and blue with her fur collar, dotted veil, and hat decorated with ostrich feathers, as she appeared on the poster of *La Revue Blanche* in 1895.

Looking at these portraits, and those of Ève Lavallière (pencil), Polaire (brush), Marcelle Linder (pen), Oscar Wilde (watercolor, which he rarely used), Suzanne Valadon (India ink and blue crayon), whose features the painter used in *La Buveuse* (The Drinker), also called *Gueule de bois* (The Hangover), we realize how the act of drawing could resemble an activity of reflection, despite the apparent rapidity of Toulouse-Lautrec's work. In a few lines he constructs the solid picture that captures our attention by the psychological lighting it projects on his model.

GRAPHIC FRENZY

If the influence of Japanese art on Lautrec is visible in his lithographs, it operated quite differently in the case of Van Gogh (pages 181, 182, 183, 184). A portrait that he did in 1887 shows old Tanguy, wearing a round hat, seated with his hands folded before him, and his back to a screen covered with Japanese prints. We recognize among the latter the classic subjects: the courtesan in a kimono, the flowering cherry tree, the inevitable Mount Fuji. Some twenty years earlier (which proves that the taste for Japanese art did not develop as late as is sometimes claimed), Manet had already used one of these prints in his portrait of Émile Zola. In Van Gogh's canvas

AUGUSTE RENOIR *France* Bather Drying Herself   Red chalk   Private Collection

they form a more important background, and Tanguy himself has almost the appearance of a Japanese man. Aside from this, however, nothing in the painting resembles their graphic style; on the contrary, we feel the beginnings, somewhat heavy and awkward, of what will soon be the Van Gogh style. Two years earlier he had discovered Japanese prints at Anvers; then, in Paris, where he met Toulouse-Lautrec, he had begun to copy Hiroshige's works.

In 1888 he arrived in Arles, from which city he wrote to his brother, Theo, that for him the South is "the equivalent of Japan." What does he mean by this? He explains in the rest of his letter: "I wish you would spend some time here; you would feel it after a while. The vision changes, you see with a more Japanese eye, you feel color differently." And among the "thousand reasons" why he has come to the South to work, he includes the following: "Looking at nature under a clearer sky can give us a better idea of the Japanese way of feeling and drawing." Thus, strangely enough, the shock he experienced under the Provençal sun, and the liberation brought him by the color of the South, are linked in his mind with a "Japanese" phenomenon.

In light of these epistolary confidences, the portrait of Père Tanguy acquires a historic significance in the painter's evolution: it shows us simultaneously, in a synthetical abridgment, Japanese art as the determining factor in a fundamental stage of this evolution, and the premature appearance of a graphic style that will not be fully developed, or attain complete power, until the following year in Provence. For Van Gogh, this was to be the pivotal point of a decisive development in his esthetics.

But how was he going to see things with "a more Japanese eye?" Like Toulouse-Lautrec, giving an unexpected rhythm to the linear movement of his composition? Like Bonnard (page 227) who, after 1890 (the year of the Exhibition of Japanese Art at the École des Beaux-Arts), suddenly decided to solve the problems of perspective and modeling by using large areas of color? Like Vuillard who, after 1893 (the year of the Utamaro-Hiroshige Exhibition in Paris), began using in his lithographs an interplay of the decorative motifs of fabrics and wallpaper, after the manner of the Ukiyo-e artists? No, and it must be admitted that Van Gogh was the least "Japanese" of the Japanese-style painters. But if we compare the drawings of his Dutch period with those of the Provençal period, we see that a graphic impulse has been given him by the knowledge of an art in which suppleness of hand and freedom of line were novelties to him. The hard steel pen was abandoned for the quill, at once more elegant and more nervous (and also closer to the brush used by Japanese artists), with which he executed several hundred ink drawings that are, as it were, more intimate versions of the work he did in Arles, Saint-Rémy, and Auvers-sur-Oise, and whose fulgurant character they retain, even without color.

Had Van Gogh seen original drawings by Japanese artists? It is quite likely, although at that time prints were better known outside Japan than drawings. They were executed with prodigious skill by wood engravers who translated with the chisel what artists had drawn. Nevertheless, not always the best prints reached France, and in any event a constant concern for decorative value detracted from the freedom and spontaneity that were the charm of the brush drawing. It is in the drawings that we find the precision of an indication, the evocative power of a few lines that represent almost nothing but are richly suggestive, the delicacy and conciseness of the India-ink strokes, especially when the drawings bear the seal of a Hokusai, the older Kuniyoshi, or a Hiroshige, to mention only those artists who belong, at least for the most part, to the nineteenth century.

All three were famous as landscapists. Hokusai (1760-1849), whose *Pilgrim Monk* is reproduced for the first time in this book (page 225), was known for his portraits of actors and pretty women before he drew his series of landscapes known as the *Thirty-six Views of Fuji*. Kuniyoshi (1797-1861), who sometimes liked to draw animals in human form, as did Bunrin and Raisho (page 224), two painters of the Shijo school, was moreover regarded as the great Ukiyo-e specialist in the drawing of fish. Although Hiroshige (1797-1858) (page 228), the author of the *One Hundred Views of Edo*, was not so great a painter as Hokusai, his landscapes, which express the poetic feelings inspired in him by rain and snow, are typical examples of the Japanese manner of observing scenes of nature. He has left us more than 5,000 engravings and beautiful brush drawings.

This brings us back to Van Gogh. We may find it strange that the painter of the sun could have been inspired by the painter of the rain, but we have proof in the form of the copy that he made of Hiroshige's *Bridge Under Rain* (V. W. van Gogh Collection, Laren). But the *Bridge Under Rain*, like the pictures shown in the portrait of Père Tanguy, is an engraving, and if we believe that the painter also had occasion to see original brush drawings by the great Japanese draftsmen, it is because many of his drawings, done with the quill, are strikingly reminiscent of their technique and dexterity (he had begun to draw and paint with great rapidity). Such are, for example, his *Vergers de Provence* and his sketches of the *Pont de l'Anglois* (Bridge at Anglois), that drawbridge near Arles similar to those that can still be seen in Holland and that were the subject of five canvases, Van Gogh having discovered in this theme a possible link between the Provençal country and a landscape familiar to him.

Thus we can continue to follow in his works the extraordinary itinerary which led him from the *Bridge Under Rain* to the *Pont de l'Anglois*, from damp Holland to sunny Provence by way of Japan. All this, however, despite the major importance of such a journey in his life, constitutes only a single episode in Van Gogh's creative activity. Unlike some artists whose drawings we studied earlier, pointing out what differentiates them from the artist's paintings, at all stages of his development Van Gogh always brought his method of drawing into line with his style of painting.

We possess drawings that date from his childhood, from the period when they were distributed as rewards to the pupils in the religious instruction classes given by his three aunts in the village of Helvoirt. Thus Van Gogh was drawing long before he studied painting. At the age of twenty he was not yet painting, but he was filling notebooks with sketches, several of which were found in 1964.

In the dreary country of the Borinage, he drew miners and coal merchants. Then he copied works by Millet and, following the latter's example, studied the peasants at work, a subject that inspired him until the end of his life. He was already almost thirty years of age when he began to paint. Between 1883 and 1885, in Nuenen, where his father was a minister, he drew, with pen, charcoal, or graphite, landscapes, a weaver at his loom, village people in their gloomy houses, women sewing or sweeping, a woman shelling peas, and people eating potatoes. In these drawings, executed with a rather heavy hand, we discover the themes and the same oppressive atmosphere of his early pictures. They became lighter and already much more res-

HENRI DE TOULOUSE-LAUTREC *France* The Barmaid
Pastel on cardboard Albi Museum, Albi

GEORGES SEURAT *France* Little Girl with Broad-Brimmed Hat Conté crayon Coll. Jacques Seligmann, New York

GEORGES SEURAT *France* Nightclub Conté crayon Municipal Museum, Amsterdam   219

220

SUZANNE VALADON *France* Portrait of Utrillo as a Child
Red chalk   Musée National d'Art Moderne, Paris

◁ SUZANNE VALADON *France* Model Pulling up her Stocking
Pastel   Collection Paul Pétridès, Paris

EDVARD MUNCH *Norway* Two Women
Watercolor Galerie Beyeler, Basel

PABLO PICASSO *Spain* Reading the Letter ▷
Charcoal and watercolor Private collection, Paris

RAISHO *Japan* A Fox Dressed as a Monk
India ink with touches of bistre Collection Janette Ostier, Paris

Katsushika Hokusai *Japan* A Pilgrim Monk Brush, India-ink wash Collection Janette Ostier, Paris

pirable in the watercolors he did in Paris, where he frequented the company of the impressionists, during 1886 and 1887.

As soon as he arrived in Arles (in 1888), his drawing changed along with his painting. In the frenzy of production that from then on was to fill the two remaining years of his life, he drew landscapes, adapting the convulsive, hallucinated style of his paintings, in which his mind seems carried away in a whirlwind of fields, trees, and suns, to the graphic technique of the quill.

Many of Van Gogh's drawings were intended for his brother, whom he kept constantly informed of the progress of his work. For the same reason, he wrote many illustrated letters to Theo. A strange graphic link is apparent between the handwriting and the drawings; word and picture stand side by side like two forms of a single visual faculty and a single thought.

Such a practice was current among many painters. Cézanne scattered sketches throughout his letters to Émile Zola. Manet decorated his letters with small watercolors; several of the letters he wrote to Isabelle Lemonnier (of whom he did six portraits, including two in pastel, in 1879) are kept in an album in the Cabinet des Dessins in the Louvre.

Gauguin (pages 173, 177, 179, 180, 187, 188, 189) carried the taste for illustrated writings still further. His *Noa-Noa* (Louvre) is a genuine book, which he wrote in collaboration with Charles Morice and which contains 182 sheets, decorated with 77 watercolors and woodcuts. The *Cahier d'Aline* (Bibliothèque d'Art et d'Archéologie of the University of Paris), another, less ambitious manuscript from his hand, and one with a deeply moving destiny, was composed on Tahiti in 1893. It contains, according to Gauguin's own description of it on the first page, "scattered notes, as isolated as dreams, and like Life itself composed of bits and pieces." A watercolor illustrating the notebook bears words in the Maori language: *Maneo Tupapau*, which can be translated as, "The Spirit of the Dead is watching." The book was intended for his daughter Aline, who died before it reached her.

Gauguin did several lithographs and woodcuts on this same theme of the Spirit of the Dead. Very often, moreover, we rediscover in his watercolors the subjects of his engravings or canvases; so the *Ève exotique* (or *la Tahitienne*) in the Musée de Grenoble, painted in 1892 during his first stay in Polynesia, appears in several drawings and woodcuts, as well as in the painting entitled *Te nave nave fenua*.

Gauguin's drawings, especially when they are direct studies from nature, are free of those spiritualist and symbolist experiments, dear to his vocation as a theoretician, which characterize many of his canvases and which were to contribute to the formation of the group called the "Nabis." However, in his studies of Brittany women, as in those done at the same period by his friend Émile Bernard (page 192) at Pont-Aven, we sometimes feel the stylistic consequences of these studies: an inclination toward a decorative simplification of forms that leads us to discover in them — and still more in the works of Paul Sérusier and Maurice Denis — the effects of *Art Nouveau*.

THE TURN OF THE CENTURY

No one, however, traveled so far along the path of the spirit of stylization as the Austrian Gustav Klimt (page 234) and the Englishman Aubrey Beardsley (page 121). The former, whose name is linked with the founding in 1897 ot the Wiener Sezession (Viennese Secession), influenced the decorative arts of his time by the ornamental frenzy of his compositions: tormented floral motifs and women emerging from a dream world of precious stones are intermingled in a mannerism in which a new form of baroque art can be seen. However, Klimt could also draw, with a simple pencil line, very pretty nudes that were unaffected by the *Art Nouveau* style.

Beardsley was exclusively a draftsman, although, being tempted by literature, and (in the words of Arthur Symons) "absolutely obsessed with the desire to be a writer," he left several traces of his taste for "artistically perverse objects," which he described in a style full of mannerisms borrowed from Oscar Wilde. The latter's somewhat conspicuous friendship, moreover, almost involved the young esthete in serious difficulties. An heir of Pre-Raphaelism, and an admirer of Hokusai and Botticelli, he perfected an esthetics of black and white by an ingenious disposition of solid areas of India ink that was admirably well suited to illustration. But his love of stylized forms, and the sophisticated refinements he brought to the graphic style of his compositions, strongly stamped his work with a *fin-de-siècle* quality.

PIERRE BONNARD *France* Misia Godebska Charcoal on cardboard Musée National d'Art Moderne, Paris

He collaborated on the *Yellow Book*, and illustrated Oscar Wilde's *Salomé*, Malory's *La Morte d'Arthur*, Théophile Gautier's *Mademoiselle de Maupin*, and Aristophanes' *Lysistrata*. His drawings, particularly for the latter, combined the most elaborate elegance with the most exaggerated eroticism, a fact that won for him the nickname of "the Fra Angelico of Satanism." A repentant sinner turned fervent Catholic, Beardsley asked that his unduly daring drawings be destroyed; they were not. He died, a victim of tuberculosis, in 1898, not yet twenty-six years of age.

At the opposite end of the spectrum from Beardsley's preciosity stands, also in the closing years of the nineteenth century, the grimacing universe of James Ensor (page 232). His works are an assertion of a vision of man that was to participate in the formation of a new artistic current, expressionism, of which Van Gogh was, in his conception of landscape alone, indisputably a precursor. In his drawings, which repeat most of the themes of his paintings and engravings, Ensor has drawn with an agitated hand grotesque creations that are incarnations of the spirit of his rebellions and obsessions: demons, phantoms, masks, skeletons, rascals, portrayed by his Flemish truculence with a dark humor.

More tragic and anguished are the drawings and lithographs of the Norwegian

ICHIRYUSAI HIROSHIGE *Japan* Landscape
Brush, India ink Collection Janette Ostier, Paris

HANS VON MARÉES *Germany* Group of Women with a Team of Horses
Red chalk   Kupferstichkabinett, Munich

Edvard Munch (page 222). The morbid expressionism and magical quality of these figures with their disturbing deformations, which he exhibited in Berlin in 1892, are quite shocking. At the same time, something found in a certain sinuosity of his favorite forms links him with the spirit of Art Nouveau, while he approaches Picasso's youthful drawings (pages 223, 229) in the "miserabilist" side of his work.

We have now seen the conjunctures of trends and ideas, as well as of contradictory movements, that were achieved by the artists who stood on the threshold of the twentieth century, as summarized in their drawings with all the clarity of a schematic demonstration. These drawings also serve as a confirmation, at the close

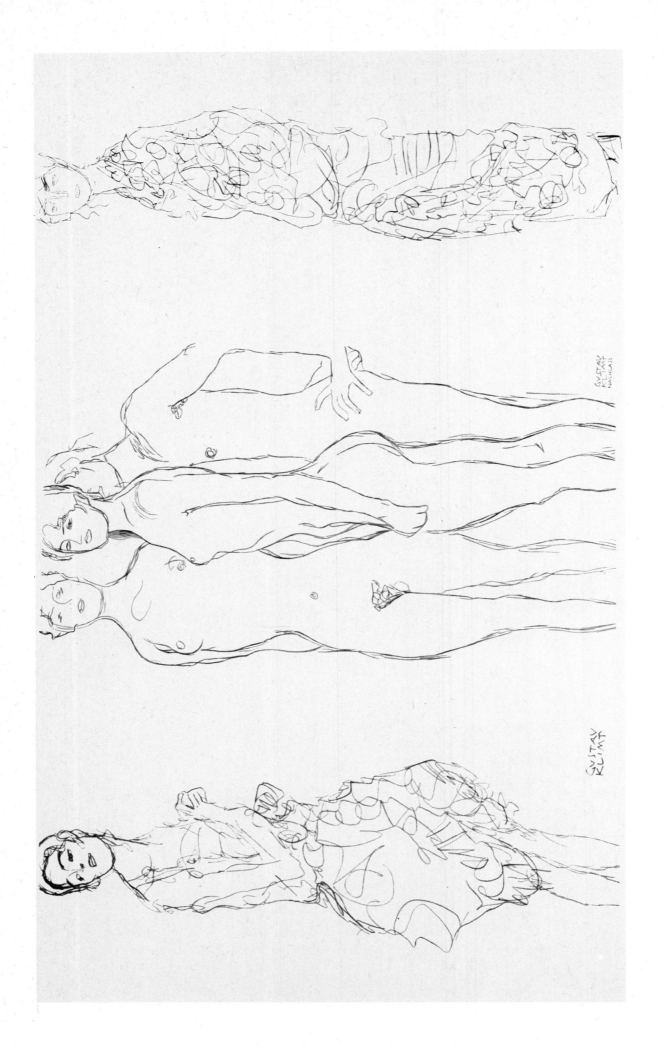

GUSTAV KLIMT *Austria* Studies of Women Pencil Albertina, Vienna

LIST OF ARTISTS
AND ILLUSTRATIONS

238

239

CONTENTS